Beyond RUBBER DUCKIES

Preparing Children for the Voyage of Life

Judy Ann Mumford
Deut 6: 5-9

DR. JUDY ANN MUMFORD

Deep River
BOOKS

Published by
Deep River Books
Sisters, Oregon
www.deepriverbooks.com

ISBN 10: 1937756939
ISBN 13: 9781937756932

Library of Congress: 2013946351

Printed in the USA

Design by Robin Black, www.InspirioDesign.com

With deep gratitude . . .

To my parents, Lewis and Edith Gutwein,
who epitomized compassionate, supportive, and loving parents.

To my husband, the father of my children,
and my best friend, Spence,
with whom I've been blessed to share the parenting journey.

To our older son, Rick, whose birth unleashed
a flood of indescribable and never-ending maternal love and joy.

To our younger son, BJ, whose unique and perceptive view of life
has inspired me immeasurably.

To God, my heavenly Father, in whose loving care I bask
and on whom I depend for life itself.

CONTENTS

PREFACE

*A*ny successful voyage requires thoughtful preparation, pragmatic planning, and unexpected adaptations along the way. The parenting journey is no exception. But no two families can, or should, follow exactly the same path. Family dynamics, individual traits, genetic influences, and internalized belief systems all have an impact on our attitudes, choices, and behaviors. As parents, we have the responsibility and privilege of thoughtfully plotting a course that best suits our family's collective and individual needs.

Beyond Rubber Duckies is designed to assist parents in promoting optimal development during the early years and laying a solid foundation for wise choices during adolescence and into adulthood. You are invited to thoughtfully, realistically, expectantly, and confidently chart your family's course through the unexplored waters that lie ahead.

INTRODUCTION

*A*s strange as it seems, this book about parenting during the early childhood years was primarily motivated by my fascination and concern with risky *adolescent* behaviors—things like reckless driving, drug use, binge drinking, and premarital (and often unprotected) sex. Attempting to counsel and console battle-weary parents led me to an impassioned search for answers to an age-old question: "Why do such smart kids make such dumb choices?"

Because adolescents themselves have taught me so much, I have included some of their comments and observations about the roots of their risky behavior. As they participated in one-on-one interviews, they openly shared their stories with me, allowing me to see the effects of varying family influences and parenting styles.

Based on my firm conviction that what parents do today has the potential to greatly affect the decisions their children make tomorrow, I present practical principles to help you develop your own philosophy of parenting. Hopefully you will be encouraged to consider, plan, and embrace the journey of parenting on which you've embarked.

Parenting is as complex as human nature itself. Just as a night-shirt's claim of "one size fits all" is called into question by a size two petite frame, only the inexperienced or naïve would recommend a predetermined, formula-type approach to raising children. No matter how sound parenting advice might appear on the surface, to be effective it must be fitted not only to each family's, but also to each child's unique characteristics and needs.

Although this book is based on empirical research, with references listed in the endnotes, I'm quite sure you're not interested in jargon-laden, technical descriptions of complex theories of human development; therefore, I provide only enough explanation to lend credibility to the connection between these ideas and your parenting. And because I assume you have limited time for reading much other than Dr. Seuss books and the instructions on children's aspirin labels, I am committed to brevity.

Hundreds of books—some with catchy titles, some that zero in on the challenges of particular stages and phases, and others that present "formulas" for parenting success—are already in print. Books on bonding, discipline, and self-esteem are but a visit to your local (or online) bookstore away. Why another book on parenting?

My hope is that every parent who picks up this book will find some tip, insight, or suggestion that will be meaningful and useful. Although I have included principles that can apply to various situations (e.g., a developmentally delayed child) and relationships (e.g., co-parenting with a former spouse), I have left discussion of specific circumstances that greatly complicate parenting to those who are better qualified than I.

You will find a common thread throughout the pages of this book: references to the Bible and the importance of a connection with Someone greater than oneself. This reflects my belief in a God who lovingly and wisely guides us through life's waters, be they peaceful or troubled.

As a daughter, sister, wife, mother and grandmother, I have experienced firsthand the joys and challenges of relationships within the family.

As a friend, I have been both the recipient and the provider of parenting counsel.

In my professional life, I have given parenting advice to parents seeking to understand temperamental and developmental issues and translate them into effective practice.

Both as a qualitative researcher and a friend of numerous teens, I have been involved in lengthy discussions with adolescents whose lives have been irreversibly altered by poor choices.

In a diverse array of roles, I have observed, examined, and contemplated child behaviors and parenting practices, attempting to make some sense of possible correlations and connections.

My personal experience has absolutely convinced me that parenting is one of life's greatest blessings. I am equally certain that it is not for the faint of heart. My desire in writing this book is to motivate, support, and encourage you, rather than offer you a ready-made map. My prayer is that the suggestions in this book will elicit a desire to chart your own individualized and gratifying course through the wide sea of parenting.

Chapter 1
SMALL BOAT, WIDE SEA

Dear Lord, be good to me.
The sea is so wide and my boat is so small.
(IRISH FISHERMAN'S PRAYER)

"No one ever said it would be easy." I don't know the origin of this phrase; I can only speculate that it was first uttered by a person in the midst of parenting. When new parents and their "precious bundle" leave the maternity ward of the local hospital, arms loaded with congratulatory balloons, flowers, and free samples of no-tears baby shampoo, they are catapulted into the world of parenting. Ready or not, here they come. Some have had no training or experience at all, some have taken an eight-week course where they've practiced changing a baby doll or teddy bear's diaper, and others have cared for younger siblings and read dozens of parenting books. However, even the most prepared can find themselves insecure and overwhelmed. I assure you, I speak from personal experience.

I had been married to my childhood sweetheart for three years, and I was ecstatic when I learned we were expecting our first child. My husband had just completed a college degree and had his first "real" job. I eagerly and happily exchanged any professional aspirations to realize my true heart's desire—becoming a mother.

In the midst of what has been called the image-making stage[1] in which one idealizes parenting, my life truly was a dream. With no regrets, I quit my job early in the pregnancy because of all-day "morning" sickness. I carried our son, during a long hot summer, two and half weeks past the predicted due date. Nevertheless, my pregnancy was filled with excited anticipation. On a very limited budget, we set up a nursery: a hand-me-down crib, a stack of cloth diapers, six handmade flannel gowns with drawstring bottoms, and a small sewing rocker and oak dresser purchased at a second-hand furniture store.

Having studied child development and read numerous parenting books and magazines, our heads, our hearts, and our home were ready for the arrival of our first child. But along with the labor pains came a rude awakening. The birthing process itself was long and difficult and, as a result of complications from anesthesia during the delivery, baby Ricky and I remained in the hospital for ten days.

The immediate mother-child bonding, which many child development experts claim is imperative for optimum child outcomes, was greatly hampered by my inability to care for our infant. Once, when my own pain made it impossible for me to feed him, the nurse accused me of not wanting to be a mother. The heartbreak I felt at that moment still brings tears to my eyes, more than 43 years later. My dreams were being crushed, and my maternal self-worth was rapidly diminishing.

Back at our small, two-bedroom apartment, physical and emotional exhaustion and sleep deprivation continued to take their toll. Although generally healthy, our tiny son was discontent and seldom slept for more than an hour at a time. My husband was incredibly loving and supportive, but he was gone each day from 7:00 a.m. until 5:30 p.m. and required at least some sleep at night.

So I struggled through the long days and longer nights smiling on the outside, at least in the presence of others, but crying on the inside.

I vividly remember dressing Ricky in an adorable blue and white sailor suit with a matching hat and propping him in the corner of the sofa. When a friend admired him, my first thought was that maybe I should give him to her. I was certain that she would be a better mother than I. Thus, with initial joyful expectations dissolving into near hopelessness, my parenting journey began.

Why, in a book whose goal is to support and encourage parents, would I begin by sharing some of my most difficult struggles? First, I want you to know that I understand the pain of feeling like a less-than-perfect parent.

Second, from my current vantage point, my experience of years of parenting has shown me how times of joy can overshadow—even totally eclipse—the times of difficulty. In spite of my early misgivings and other bumps along the way, I cannot imagine anyone feeling more fortunate to be a mother.

Third, I believe it is more common than we are prone to admit for parents to feel as if they are navigating a very wide sea in a very small boat. Parents need to know that feeling stymied, incompetent, and alone is relatively commonplace and is nothing of which to be ashamed.

Finally, and most importantly, just as surely as I can admit my inadequacies and challenges as a parent, I can point to One who has always provided the strength and direction I need. I have counted heavily on scriptural promises such as "Those who hope in the LORD will renew their strength"[2] and "If any of you lacks wisdom, you should ask God, who gives generously."[3] Much as sailors can look to the North Star as a consistently accurate compass, we can trust Him to guide our tiny, turmoil-prone boats.

Chapter 2

CHARTING THE COURSE

Make your work to be in keeping with your purpose.
(LEONARDO DA VINCI)[1]

W e love our children and, of course, we have high
hopes for them. We hope they will maximize their
God-given aptitudes and minimize their seeming
deficiencies. We hope they will make wise choices regarding relationships, educational opportunities, and careers. I remember
that, as a preschooler, one of our sons decided he wanted to be a
garbage collector some day. Although I respected the profession, I
encouraged him to keep his options open.

As we envision our young children growing up to be all they can
be, we must remind ourselves that dreams do not magically turn
into reality. Perhaps this reality is what Plutarch had in mind when
he so eloquently stated, "No man ever wetted clay and then left it,
as if there would be bricks by chance and fortune." Likewise, when
a man and woman conceive a child, how foolish to assume that a life
of meaning and purpose will automatically unfold! But many of the
parents of the more than four million babies born in our country
each year have no map, no compass, no specific destination, and
little comprehension of the rigors of the journey ahead.

It's not as if any of us would intentionally leave our children's future to chance. But sometimes the immediacy of the moment—runny noses, messy diapers, untied shoes—robs us of sufficient time and energy to reflect on the impact of our daily actions and decisions on the adult our child will one day become. How do we ensure that our children's lives don't get lost in the shuffle of living?

When we see a bumper sticker announcing that there's "precious cargo on board," we can assume the cargo is a very tiny person strapped into a disproportionately large, well-padded car seat. Completely dependent on the big person behind the steering wheel in the front seat, the child has no concerns about the trip or the destination. But can our children look to us just as confidently when it comes to the challenging journey of life? Are they safely strapped in and confident that there's someone older and wiser behind the wheel?

GOAL-SETTING

When it comes to goal-setting, a well-worn adage comes to mind. The phrase, "If you aim at nothing, you'll hit it," can be aptly applied to parenting. We need a target, a goal, a sense of direction for ourselves as well as for our children. As Thomas Carlyle stated, "The man without a purpose is like a ship without a rudder—a waif, a nothing, no man."

Sure, we all have some general goals for our children, an idea of what we want them to do and be. We want them to be happy and healthy. But how can we, with our very human ideals and perspective, look beyond the obvious and align our goals for our children with God's purposes for each of us? Let me share with you a Bible verse that helped me organize my thoughts and served as a model for my hopes, plans, and daily prayers for our sons. "Jesus grew in wisdom and stature, and in favor with God and man."[2] This verse encompasses the intellectual, physical, spiritual, and

social-emotional development of the perfect God-man and provides us with a structure for considering our hopes and dreams for
our children.

I have used the Luke 2:52 blueprint as a prayer guide since our
sons were infants, and I now pray for our grandchildren in the
same way. I pray daily that they will mature in wisdom, stature,
favor with God, and favor with man. I elaborate on each of these
areas, adapting my prayers to the persons, current situations, challenges, needs, and opportunities in their lives.

Needless to say, as our sons grew and changed, so did my prayers.
My prayers that a three-year-old would understand what it means to
love Jesus eventually became prayers that a 13-year-old would understand what it means for Jesus to love him. My prayers that a six-year-
old's T-ball injuries would heal quickly were changed to prayers that
a 16-year-old's driving would result in no injuries. My prayers that
a two-year-old wouldn't bite his best friend were replaced by prayers
that a 12-year-old would choose his best friend wisely.

Not only did my aspirations for our children give direction to
my prayers, but my prayers, in turn, shaped my aspirations. As I
prayed each day that our sons would "love Jesus more than anyone
or anything else," I considered whether there were indications of
maturation in this area. I also contemplated the effectiveness with
which I was fulfilling my parental role by instilling and modeling a belief system to guide their thoughts and actions throughout
their lives.

My prayers reflected not only my passionate desire to see our
sons grow as Jesus did, but also my feelings of inadequacy as a parent. I continually asked for God's strength, wisdom, and direction and prayed that *my* plans for my children would be consistent
with *His* plans for them. It became very evident that goal-setting not
only provided direction for my children; it served to challenge and
refine me as a parent as well.

PARENTAL ROLE-MODELING

Think for a moment about these words of Francis of Assisi: "Preach always, but if necessary use words."[3] The Apostle Paul also emphasized actions, not words, when he wrote, "Be imitators of God . . . and walk in love."[4] Do we want our children to be Christlike? If so, *we* must imitate Him because, whether we like it or not, our children will imitate us. Think for a moment about the ways in which you emulate your own parents—perhaps your penchant for peanut butter and banana sandwiches, your passion for the downtrodden, or your political convictions. After all is said and done, much of charting the course for our children is dependent on our leading the way by *modeling* the attitudes and behaviors we want them to adopt.

Here's a simplistic example: If my goal is that my young child learns to respect authority and follow rules, I probably shouldn't grab his tiny hand and rush him across the street while the "no walking" sign is blinking. Explaining to him that it is "okay" because no cars are coming is pointless; situational ethics are far beyond his level of cognitive functioning.

My husband learned this lesson through experience when our son resolutely stood on the curb until the "walk" icon appeared, despite his father's coaxing to proceed. Although children's development is a gradual, long-term process, it is formed by seemingly insignificant daily behaviors and decisions, which can set precedents, serve as examples, and lead to consequences that will ultimately shape their lives.

The following questions may be helpful as we contemplate what our children are observing in us:

- Do my children hear me speak in words and tones that I want them to imitate?
- Do I model behaviors consistent with what I expect and desire from my children?

- Do my words and actions impart a consistent message?
- If my children were to use five adjectives to describe me, what would those adjectives be? How do they compare with the adjectives I hope will describe them when they are adults?

Moses, the God-appointed leader of the Israelites, certainly understood the importance of parental role-modeling. He had seen a generation of people make a series of terrible mistakes by questioning, doubting, and betraying their God. As a result, all of his generation eventually died in the barren wilderness instead of being able to enjoy the lush Promised Land.

In Deuteronomy 6, Moses is grooming the next generation and undoubtedly hoping for much better results. As he commands them to "Love the LORD your God with all your heart and with all your soul and with all your strength," he first speaks about the importance of their having a personal belief in God, telling them the commandments should be "on [their] hearts"[5] Then he strongly emphasizes the importance of parental role-modeling: "Impress [these commandments] on your children. Talk about them when you sit at home and when you walk along the road, when you lie down and when you get up."[6]

Tying the commandments on their hands symbolized God's control over their behaviors; binding them on their foreheads represented God's control over their thoughts, and writing them on the doorframes of their houses and gates proclaimed to all that their purpose in life was to serve God. Modeling a godly life is clearly a key component in the transmission of a belief system from one generation to the next.

I am also reminded of another biblical character, Joshua, who provides a great model of determining (and publicly declaring) his intentions. As leader of the Israelites, he strongly exhorts them to "fear the LORD and serve him with all faithfulness."[7] But he quickly acknowledges that each person must make his or her own choice, as he adds, "But if serving the LORD seems undesirable to you, then choose for yourselves this day whom you will serve."[8]

Joshua then speaks definitively on behalf of the entity for whom he is ultimately responsible, his own family. "As for me and my household, we will serve the LORD,"[9] he proclaims. Although it's simple to *say* that we have decided to "serve the Lord," in reality our daily choices are the true indicator of which gods we have chosen—not only for ourselves, but for our family as well. Decisions regarding the people with whom we associate, the influences to which we are exposed, the activities in which we are involved, and the responsibilities we assume all give direction to the course of our lives.

STAYING ON COURSE

One of the best incentives for steadily steering our children toward predetermined goals is understanding the critical importance of the task at hand. Researcher Judith Harris raised eyebrows not only in the world of academia but also in society at large when she challenged the "nurture assumption," that is, that the way a person parents his or her child has a great influence on how the child turns out. Harris' personal experience and research led her to assert that we need to stop believing that parents have crucial or long-lasting effects on their children.[10]

As you might guess, Harris' and my perception of parenting are quite dissimilar. To be fair to Harris, few if any students of behavioral sciences would refute her contention that vastly differing parenting styles may lead to similar child outcomes. Further, similar parenting sometimes results in vastly different child outcomes.

However, the fact that there is no guaranteed link between child outcome and parenting style does not lead me to willingly allow someone else to usurp my role as my child's primary influence.

Rather, given all the other potential influences, it increases my resolve to fulfill what I believe to be my responsibility as a parent: to plan for my child's future, to navigate the parenting waters with a dogged sense of determination and purpose, and to never, ever abandon ship.

Chapter 3

EMBARKING ON THE JOURNEY

From small beginnings come great things.
(American Proverb)

In my mind, a necessary component of any discussion of child development or parenting is recognizing the critical importance of children's first experiences. As providers and protectors, parents are largely responsible for what their young children see, hear, feel, touch, and taste. Think for a moment about an infant's total helplessness and dependency. Does he go to sleep with background sounds of soothing music or a violent movie? Is he swathed in a soft blanket, or are his tiny arms and legs left dangling and exposed to the elements? Are his wakening whimpers met with a sensitive, reassuring voice, or is he ignored until his piercing cries become intolerable to his caregiver?

The significance and potential consequences of a child's early impressions, interactions, relationships, and training cannot be overstated. As we set sail with our young child, what transpires in the first few furlongs sets the stage for the journey ahead.

Plato certainly understood the implications of early experiences, when he said:

The beginning is the most important part of any work, especially in the case of a young and tender thing; for that is the time at which the character is being formed and the desired impression is more readily taken. Shall we just carelessly allow children to hear any casual tales which may be devised by casual persons, and to receive ideas into their minds the very opposite of those which we would wish them to have?[1]

Although childhood educators and researchers have long recognized and acknowledged the importance of a child's early experiences, over the past few decades findings in the scientific world have greatly furthered our understanding of this phenomenon. We now know that a brain's "hardwiring," connecting of the neurons, occurs during a child's first few years. Pathways in the brain, developed through either positive or negative experiences, become strong and permanent with frequent use; conversely, they become weak or even extinct with infrequent use.

As an example, if a toddler's teary appeal for comfort when he skins his knees is consistently met with the admonition, "You need to be tough!" the connection in his brain that equates demonstration of emotions with weakness will become strong. This association will eventually affect his reaction to his own emotions and foster insensitivity to the physical and emotional pain of others. On the other hand, if a skinned knee is met by an exaggerated display of sympathy and concern, his brain will interpret any sort of physical discomfort as trauma deserving much attention and drama.

Related to wiring of the brain, the term "internal working model" describes brain imprints that determine a child's perception of himself and others. The internal working models of babies who experience an affectionate, fostering environment assure them they are lovable, acceptable, and worthy. The nurturing adults in their lives are seen as dependable and responsive to their needs. These children's early beliefs about themselves and others enable them to develop into sensitive, trusting, and respectful persons.

Once again, the opposite is also true. When children are angry, fearful, and distrustful, we can surmise that their internal models have convinced them they have little worth and others are not to be trusted.

In an intriguing application of knowledge about brain development, one parenting perspective emphasizes the correlation between early experiences and the functioning of various parts of the brain: the brain stem, the limbic system, and the prefrontal lobe.[2] Very young children, as well as some older children and even adults who feel physically threatened, respond to stimuli in a survival ("fight or flight") mode. Arousal and survival responses, which originate in the brain stem, typically include aggression (kicking, hitting, pushing, biting) and withdrawal.

Children raised in insensitive and uncaring environments remain stuck in the brain stem mode, sometimes for life. Someone functioning at this level readily succumbs to self-centered, thoughtless, knee-jerk responses with no regard to potential consequences or others' well-being. Sadly, many adults who find themselves behind bars have never learned to respond to difficulties at a level beyond the brain stem. Conversely, children who live in a context of safety and security learn to move from brain stem responses to a higher functioning level of the brain, the limbic system.

Much as brain stem reactions are physical, the limbic system's responses are emotional in nature.[3] Sobbing, whining, pouting and verbal outbursts are emotional responses to sadness, perceived inequity, and unfulfilled wants or needs. Validation of children's feelings, through empathy and understanding, helps them learn the art of successfully identifying, demonstrating, and controlling their emotions.

As is true of physical responses, some people never move past emotionally volatile responses to stimuli. Although appropriately venting emotions is necessary and even therapeutic at times, exclusively emotionally-driven decisions and behaviors lead to undue stress, conflicts in relationships, and feelings of helplessness. Beyond emotions, the next level of functioning involves the brain's frontal lobe, which is capable of consistently sound decision-making.

The frontal lobe is the area of the brain in which thinking and problem-solving occur.[4] Young children who are fighting over the same toy can be taught to take turns, thus resolving conflict without hitting (a brain stem response) or yelling, "That's not fair!" (a limbic system response). When we teach children how to react to stimuli in appropriate ways, we are encouraging the development of an invaluable tool for life: self-control, or self-regulation.

When our sons were very young, one of the songs they learned (and we all sang around the house) described self-control in very simplistic terms. "Self-control is just controlling myself. It's listening to my heart, and doing what is smart. Self-control is the very best way to go, so I think that I'll control myself."[5]

Yes, self-control really *is* the "best way to go," not only for children but for adults as well. Remember, what we model as parents— e.g., whether we respond to life's challenges and disappointments with composure and control or with an obvious lack thereof—plays a major role in whether our children will function primarily at the brain stem, limbic system, or frontal lobe level.

As our little ones begin the journey of life, our privilege and responsibility is to attempt to ensure that their early experiences equip them with constructive hardwiring of the brain, affirming rather than condemning internal working models, and the ability to respond in an appropriate manner to various stimuli.

Chapter 4
CAMARADERIE AMONG THE CREW

It is better to bind your children to you by a feeling of respect,
and by gentleness, than by fear.

(TERENCE)[1]

While other parts of this book address the issue of external influences on our family, the focus in this section is on the internal: the relationships, interactions, and dynamics within the home. Much as a ship's crew must function as a team to keep the vessel on course, the family unit must be characterized by a sense of teamwork that is dependent on mutual cooperation and support.

Specifically, families need to function in such a way that *all* members feel unconditionally loved, respected, and accepted. These factors are so intertwined that there is no obvious way to delineate them. All three seem to grow out of a sense of connectedness among family members, which I refer to here as cohesion.

COHESION

Several years ago I developed a seminar for parents of adolescents that I called "Parent-Adolescent Connectedness: Protection against Unacceptable Adolescent Behaviors." This seminar was driven by something I thought parents need to know: Research findings consistently suggest that when parents and their adolescents have warm and caring relationships, teens are less likely to engage in delinquency, violence, and substance use.[2, 3] On the flip side, teens' perception of low parental caring is associated with unhealthy weight control, suicide attempts, body dissatisfaction, depression, and low self-esteem.[4]

While the above-mentioned research found that family cohesion lessened the chances that teens would engage in destructive behaviors, my own research unveiled a complementary theme: Cohesion was the *missing* component in the homes of many teens who, as a result of poor choices and strained relationships, were living at a residential facility away from their families. One teen described the family dynamics with these words: "Everyone would just kind of do their own thing in a way, so it's kind of like the environment was just, you'd take care of yourself." After a run-in with the law, another dramatically demonstrated her dislike for her family by choosing to be arrested and spend time in jail rather than go home with her parents.

The point is not whether the relationships in these homes were actually as strained and distant as the teens perceived or their comments would imply. Rather, we must remember that their perceptions and feelings were real to them and likely played a role in the way they distanced themselves from and eventually rebelled against their parents. Although explaining human behavior is anything but an exacting art, we *can* say that as family cohesion decreases, the probability that children will engage in harmful behavior appears to increase.

When introducing this topic, I used the word "mutual" to describe the desired cooperation and support within a family. As we know, relationships are bi-directional—both parents and children contribute to the family dynamics in positive and/or negative ways. And, as they become older, children have a greater responsibility to think of others and not just themselves. We don't expect a three-year-old to come to the kitchen during meal preparation and ask if he can do anything to help. It is not unrealistic, however, to expect an eight-year-old to do so. That being said, we must remember that the duty of modeling and promoting positive qualities clearly falls on the shoulders of the parents.

UNCONDITIONAL LOVE

Unconditional love can be described as a love that we do nothing to deserve and can do nothing to destroy. Even though it may be difficult to grasp or explain, we all know that kind of love is something that all humans innately crave. This was evident as I talked with teens who were attempting to fill an emotional void by searching for love outside the family parameters.

One teen told me, "My parents weren't always there . . . and I could never really tell if they loved me. I needed to go somewhere else to find that . . . [I was] just searching for someone to take care of me."

She sensed that a critical component was missing in her relationship with her parents. The absence of unconditional love, at least in her perception, made her particularly vulnerable to peer influence that led her down a destructive path.

What does it mean for parents to love their children unconditionally? I believe the following statement captures its essence: "Before becoming a mother I had a hundred theories on how to bring up children. Now I have seven children and only one theory: Love them, especially when they least deserve it."[5]

We as parents don't have to be reminded to love our babies as they sleep peacefully, clinging to their teddy bears or blankets for security in our absence. We adore our three-year-olds as they emerge from their preschool classroom with their bright red "I love Daddy" backpack dangling from their tiny shoulders. We proudly sit in the bleachers as our six-year-olds don seemingly disproportionately large batting helmets and step to the plate. We beam with pride as our eight-year-old sings in the church's Angel Choir. Loving the lovely, the adorable, the cute, or the charming isn't much of a challenge.

It is precisely at the point that effortless love stops, that supernatural (i.e., unconditional) love starts. The latter never fails, or even wavers, due to circumstances (no matter how trying) or performance (no matter how disappointing). The Bible simplistically yet eloquently describes unconditional love as the "more excellent way."[6] Love *is* patient, kind, trusting, hopeful, and persevering. Love *is not* rude, self-seeking, or easily angered.[7] Unconditional love is unrestricted, undeserved, and absolute.

Our demonstration of love toward our children during their early years has a great impact on many aspects of their development, including their sense of worth. Accepting and valuing them, and thus promoting their self-esteem, is truly one of the best gifts we can give our children. In fact, a healthy self-esteem was a quality conspicuously and consistently absent from the troubled teens with whom I spoke. Whether their labels originated with themselves or others, I do not know. However, with few exceptions the respondents perceived themselves negatively. I sadly listened to them use terms including "dysfunctional," "bad," "the one who gets in trouble," "pretty messed up," "not good," "not typical," and "not normal" to describe themselves. Although it is difficult to specify the exact connection among a perceived absence of parental love, troubled behaviors, and self-deprecating notions, a seeming link cannot be ignored.

Using the term "social mapping," one psychologist uses the following analogy to describe children's representations of themselves and their worlds: "Some children see themselves as powerful, secure countries, surrounded by allies. Others see themselves as poor little islands, surrounded by an empty ocean or hostile enemies."[8]

This concept of a child's need for love and security is poignantly illustrated by the childhood experience of a dear friend of mine. When he was 12, his family began to disintegrate. His mother's mental breakdown led to her being institutionalized and he and his siblings were taken to a children's home. His parents subsequently divorced and he remained in the residential facility for two years. He recalls,

> By the second year I was very unhappy and really hated the superintendent—a harsh, unloving man—and the whole experience. I was taking Spanish that year in school and combining that with my unhappiness I invented a hide-a-way world for myself called the Republica del Sabado or the Republic of Saturday. I was the only citizen of this republic and I could escape there into my own dream world. This world was so important to me that eventually I found a small spot in the woods behind the barn where I staked out an area to provide an actual physical location for my Republic.[9]

In the absence of a home that provided the loving refuge that all children crave, this imaginative and resourceful young teen created his own country to which he could escape.

Parental love, given freely and unconditionally, provides protection against children's foes such as low self-esteem, fear, anger, and loneliness. As parents, we strive to love our children to this depth, but do we ever fall short? If you'd ask me whether I have always loved my children, I would probably somewhat indignantly reply, "Of course!" To add credibility to my definitive answer, I would admit that there have been times when I haven't *liked* our sons, but I certainly have always *loved* them.

Unfortunately, if I compare my thoughts and actions with the I Corinthians 13 standards of patience, kindness, trust, hope, and perseverance, it becomes all too obvious that I have failed—rather miserably at times—to love my children as I ought. Just looking at the very first condition of absolute love—patience—is a painful reality check for me.

Perhaps you can identify with my shortcomings in this matter. If so, rather than let missed opportunities of the past cause undue regrets and discouragement, we can learn from them and move on with determination to do better. Each day provides a myriad of opportunities to love our children unconditionally. As a means of assessment, let's ask ourselves these questions.

- On a scale of 1–10, how do I rate myself on each of the following 1 Corinthians 13 qualities as I interact with my children:

    patient

    kind

    protective

    trusting

    hopeful

    persevering

    not rude

    not self-centered

    not easily angered

- What specific steps can I take to improve any of the above qualities I've rated 7 or lower?

- Are there certain recognizable, predictable patterns in my less-than-loving responses? (For example, am I more likely to be rude when I'm rushed or preoccupied?) If so, how can I change these patterns?

- Has there been a specific, recent situation when I was unable to show my child unconditional love? If so, why? If a similar situation were to arise again, would I attempt to respond differently? What would help me do so?

- In what specific, recent situation was I able to demonstrate love in spite of my child's behavior? What impact did my response have on my child?

- Do I attempt to treat all my children the same when it comes to demonstrations of love? If not, why?

- Do my actions toward my children promote or inhibit the development of healthy self-esteem?

Before we leave the topic of love, I would like to address my concern about a growing trend I have observed among parents of young children. I believe the term "unconditional love" is much too frequently equated with an indulgent parenting style.

Let's pause a moment on this point to consider how society has glorified the accumulation of things. Sadly, many parents have fallen into the bigger-and-better trap and believe they are "demonstrating love" by buying their children stuff. Children have learned the art of masterfully controlling their parents' wallets by preying on their weaknesses, such as the apparent inability of some parents to deny their children their requests.

The supposition that affection is demonstrated through the giving of material possessions is a notion that has a great, and potentially devastating, impact on young children's future beliefs and value systems. Where and why did we begin believing that a trip to the store should routinely involve buying something for our children?

About now, some of you are wondering if I am totally unaware that exchanging gifts has been identified and justifiably recognized as a "love language."[10] You argue, legitimately, that while some people feel loved through verbal expressions or acts of service, others prefer receiving something they can see and touch. But hear me out. The concept of love languages reinforces and complements, rather than negates, my point. A gift, given at an appropriate time and prompted by love, is a wonderful expression of affection.

By contrast, buying stuff for our children simply because they nag until we are exhausted, or because we feel guilty if we don't, is not really demonstrating love at all. On the contrary, it may be encouraging character patterns of self-centeredness, self-indulgence and ingratitude. When children's appetites become insatiable, they view their wishes as entitlements. This sort of thinking, instilled in the early years and repeatedly reinforced, becomes increasingly difficult to reverse over time. Often, the most loving thing we can say to our children is an unequivocal "no."

RESPECT

As noted earlier, loving children unconditionally and treating them respectfully are quite inseparable, at least in my mind. One thing that never ceases to amaze and dismay me is the manner in which some parents treat their children at shopping malls, fast-food restaurants, supermarkets, and playgrounds. No doubt you, as well as I, have observed parents yelling at, threatening, and sometimes even slapping their children.

Often, a parental tirade is induced by something as innocent as a child accidentally knocking merchandise off a shelf or wading through an irresistibly inviting mud puddle. At other times, children's behaviors are truly unacceptable. Even then, poor behavior is often precipitated by physical needs such as hunger, fatigue, or boredom that might have been circumvented by sensitive parenting. Regardless of the cause of the behavior, children should be dealt with in a perceptive and caring manner. Based on what I see in public, I shudder at the thought of what might happen behind closed doors.

Perhaps parents who engage in berating their offspring have forgotten that children are people too. Of course, young children are small and immature—that's an inherent and inevitable part of their current developmental stage. But in no way does that mean they are inferior human beings or that their self-worth is unaffected by how others treat them.

Further, children should never be manipulated by a parent on a power trip. A dad shouldn't demand that his son play football because it will give his father something to brag about at the office.

A mother shouldn't expect her daughter to satisfy her unfulfilled dreams to be a gymnast.

As we continually show respect to our children, we demonstrate our conviction that they have feelings and worth. Thus, we support their efforts to become confident and self-regulating individuals. Respecting children means no coercion, no name-calling, no yelling, and no belittling. What it does *not* mean—and what I am not suggesting—is that parents have no authority or right to respond decisively in the face of their children's inappropriate behaviors.

ACCEPTANCE

Along with loving and respecting our children, accepting their uniqueness is absolutely essential to their emotional well-being. As frustrating and complex as it seems, a particular parenting style may be perfectly suited to one of our children and be just as ill-suited to another. Do we merely give intellectual assent to our children's differences, or does our parenting demonstrate that we truly understand the concept?

Children are born with innate traits—artistic giftedness, a melancholy predisposition, intellectual prowess, or stubbornness. Even though it is obvious that no two children are alike, we still struggle to parent in a way that truly considers and accepts their individual differences. Often, when parents are frustrated with (or even embarrassed by) a child, they will console themselves and assure others with comments such as, "She's so different from her sister." Acceptance of our children is not synonymous with acceptance of their inappropriate behaviors. But is does mean adamantly rejecting the belief that one child is an inferior person simply because she does not fit our definition of a "model" child. We're human so, of course, at times we will wonder, *Why can't she be like her sister?* or *How can she be so difficult?* But this is a message that none of our children should ever even sense, let alone hear. What children need, on the other hand, is consistent affirmation of their uniqueness and worth.

One of the most obvious differences among children is in their temperaments. Like other biological traits, children have no control over the temperaments with which they are born. This knowledge alone should be enough to make us more accepting of our child's unique qualities and more willing to make necessary adaptations to his or her needs.

Our children come into the world with a particular set of characteristics that affect how they feel inside and how they view the world around them. Does your baby startle easily or calmly relax despite loud noises? Does your toddler quietly observe peers or aggressively and actively take charge? Does your preschooler bound out of bed in the morning ready to take on the world or sleepily drag out of bed, expecting the world to meet his needs? Children's temperaments determine whether they are active or passive, attentive or distractible, noisy or quiet, cautious or eager, adaptable or resistant, and happy or melancholy.

Although some temperaments are more challenging for parents, we must remember that every child, just as every adult, has both strengths and limitations. The key to raising healthy, well-adjusted children is to attempt to adapt their environments to best meet their individual needs. Bottom line? The contexts in which our children live either enhance their assets and diminish their liabilities, or vice versa.

We would be somewhat less than honest to deny that unhappy and uncooperative children greatly try the souls of even the most patient, committed, and optimistic parents. But let me offer some encouragement to those of you who believe that some of the not-too-positive adjectives apply to your child.

First, biology is only one factor that determines a child's development. As noted above, the environments in which our children are raised play an immense role in determining who they become. As a very simple example, providing a shy child with opportunities to socialize helps her to become more self-confident and outgoing.

Second, qualities that are frustrating and difficult to deal with in our children may actually serve them very well. We all know of strong-willed children who accomplish great feats, highly sensitive children who exhibit amazing creativity, and slow-to-adapt children who stand firm in the face of peer influence.

The phrase "intelligent empathy" is a very meaningful concept when it comes to accepting our children's temperaments and adapting accordingly. Based on truly trying to understand our children, intelligent empathy is "firmly believing that what the child does and says makes sense if approached from the child's point of view."[11]

This is not an easy concept to put into practice. Consider how difficult it is to step back and objectively assess a two-year-old's reasons for repeatedly attempting to bathe the new puppy in the toilet bowl.

Taking the concept of accepting our children a step further, we must not attempt to fit them into some preformed mold that satisfies our aspirations, pride, and concept of ideal. Our plans, hopes, and dreams for the future must be continually tempered by a realistic appraisal of our child's capabilities, needs and preferences, and the focus must be his or her ultimate good. Sadly, many adolescents and adults bear psychological scars resulting from their parents' efforts to force them to become someone they weren't meant to be. Always falling short of parental expectations, they live their lives feeling unfulfilled, thwarted, insignificant, and maybe even worthless.

Mutual love, acceptance, and respect form the foundation of a healthy family. Without these qualities, a family bears some similarities to a ship that is aimlessly adrift while it's egocentric, stubborn, and arrogant crew members are consumed with self-serving agendas.

Chapter 5
DECIPHERING MORSE CODE

*The most important thing in communication is
to hear what isn't being said.*
(Peter F. Drucker)[1]

*F*ew of us would deny that communication lies at the heart of relationships. After more than 46 years of marriage, my husband and I still frequently find ourselves communicating poorly with each other. As we attempt to unravel misunderstandings, I'm always amazed at the discrepancy between what I said ("Make sure you pick out a nice bunch of lettuce") and what he heard ("Don't buy lettuce unless it's nice"). When I'm in the midst of preparing for dinner guests, this can be problematic.

Whether it is between spouses, parent and child, employer and employee, friends or siblings, effective communication is a key to understanding and accepting others. In this chapter, we will discuss some principles that can help facilitate constructive communication between parents and their children.

One of our sons developed verbal skills at a particularly early age. He chattered incessantly as a preschooler, providing running commentaries on everything within his small world of experience and asking endless "why" questions. He was especially talkative at the dinner table, in the presence of what he perceived to be a captive audience. I recall that at times his stories were quite lengthy and disjointed, and his impromptu "jokes" weren't very humorous.

But what I remember most is how intensely important it was to him to have everyone's undivided attention when he was speaking. If he were interrupted, his eyes would well with tears, readily revealing his sense of dismay. I regret that I wasn't always patient and attentive as our young son tried out his budding communication skills. In hindsight, listening to him should have been a much higher priority than making sure the green beans were passed or the table was cleared promptly.

Listening doesn't always seem to come naturally, a reality that enhances rather than lessens its value. Effectively listening to our young children establishes a critical precedent for connecting with them as teens. As I've talked to adolescents whose relationships with their parents were strained—if not severed—a common theme continually emerged: Communication simply was not good. Let me share some examples.

Teens used the following terms to describe the communication styles in their families: "a dull roar," "yelling," and "high-pitched screaming." Others indicated that conversation with their parents of any sort—good or bad—was scarce and/or superficial. One said succinctly: "We didn't communicate at all. They were just two people that I lived with."

Effective and constructive communication between any two people involves both receiving and sending messages. We will begin with a discussion of receiving messages.

RECEIVING OUR CHILDREN'S MESSAGES

The first principle for receiving messages is stated very succinctly in the Bible: "Everyone should be quick to listen."[2] As alluded to earlier, listening seems to run counter to human nature. How do we measure up as parents? One author writes,

Determining how effective you are as a listener takes a great deal of honesty and humility. You have to be willing to quiet down and listen to yourself as you jump in and interrupt someone. Or you have to be a little more patient and observe yourself as you walk away, or begin thinking of something else, before the person you are speaking to has finished.[3]

Listening to our children requires us to give of two things we consider very valuable—our time and our attention. Realizing that the first few seconds set the tone for any conversation, we need to discipline ourselves to send an unequivocal message when our children begin speaking: I am listening.

This requires making eye contact and conveying with our body language that we are ready to hear whatever they are about to say. Failure to do so may send a very insensitive albeit unintended message: I don't care about what you are saying. The following statement seems to put the whole concept of listening in perspective: "The first duty of love is to listen."[4] What a great reminder of its importance in the context of relationships.

Parents are rightfully excited when their babies begin making their first sounds. We prompt and encourage (and report to anyone who will listen) every attempt at speech. We are particularly delighted with any semblance of "mama" or "dada." But once children's speech becomes commonplace and profuse, listening becomes increasingly difficult. By the time many children are preadolescents, they have begun saying things we don't want to hear in a manner in which we don't want them to speak. Although we know that the importance of listening never diminishes, it seems the ability and desire to do so decrease dramatically as our children grow up.

As adolescents talked with me, frustration with their parents regarding the matter of listening was evident. They commented about their parents' "selective hearing" and interrupting rather than listening before asking questions or giving advice.

Besides listening—carefully, that is—we need to listen beyond our children's words and attempt to determine what they are feeling. Throughout the New Testament, Jesus models this sort of listening. For example, the Bible records the story of Jesus being surrounded by a crowd of people at the home of two sisters, Mary and Martha. Many people had come to hear Him teach and Martha was busy preparing food and attending to the needs of their guests.

Meanwhile, Mary was attentively sitting at Jesus' feet. Feeling overwhelmed and annoyed, Martha asked, "Lord, don't you care that my sister has left me to do the work by myself? Tell her to help me!" In Jesus' response, He identified and acknowledged her feelings: "'Martha, Martha,' the Lord answered, 'you are worried and upset about many things.'"[5] By this statement, He both validated her feelings and helped her to recognize the source of her frustration.

As parents, we need to become adept at listening for what our children are attempting to convey. For example, should a statement like "I don't ever want to play baseball again" be taken at face value? Or, should it possibly be interpreted as "I felt really embarrassed today when I let the ball go over my head," or "You need to tell me that you think I'm doing okay at third base," or "Some guys on the team are making fun of me and I don't want to be around them." Depending on what our child is actually saying, a response of "Don't be silly. Of course you want to play!" may indicate that we aren't really listening at all.

Years ago in the waiting room of a dentist's office, I heard a conversation that, unfortunately, seemed to typify failure of a parent to listen to her son and his feelings. The young boy, whom I guessed to be about four, was sitting in the chair next to his mother. She was quite engrossed in reading a magazine; by contrast, he had nothing to distract or entertain himself. After sitting quietly for a few minutes, he asked his mother a simple question, "Is it my turn?" No response. With slightly increased intensity, he asked again, "Is it my turn yet?" And then, a bit louder and higher pitched, he tried again. "When's it going to be my turn, huh?" Silence.

Perhaps he realized that asking that question was futile, so he changed to a different, even more pressing issue that was obviously causing him concern. Looking intently into her face, in spite of the fact that her eyes had been riveted on the magazine since the beginning of this one-sided dialogue, he asked, "Is he going to pull out all my teeth?" Predictably, there was no response. Still politely, but with a tone that could no longer be ignored, he tried once again to get some information from his mother. "Is he going to pull out all my teeth?" Without glancing up, the mother shook her head and the small boy slumped back into the chair, apparently willing to retreat within himself and contemplate what might be.

At that moment, I wanted so desperately to pull that little boy up on my lap, hug him tightly, and quiet his trepidation. He was asking great "when" and "what" questions, indicating that he had the cognitive ability to process more information than he had been given. So, why hadn't the mother made some effort to inform and reassure him? Couldn't she hear the distress in his voice? What, if anything, had she told him before they arrived at the dentist's office? How simple it would have been, I thought, for her to briefly explain what was—and what was not—likely to happen. How simple it would have been to answer his questions and calm his anxiety. How simple for her to suggest he pick out a child's book that she could read to him, thus diverting his attention while he waited. How much effort would it have taken for her to give him a hug? Surely she could tell that he desperately needed comforting.

How easy for me to sit across the waiting room and think poorly of that mother, wanting to snatch the little boy and compensate for her apparent deficiencies. I will never know why this mother seemed so insensitive. There might have been "justifiable" reasons.

Perhaps she had already told him a thousand times (at least in her mind) what was going to happen—or that she didn't *know* what was going to happen. Perhaps she had trained herself to totally tune out his incessant jabber, having determined that was a better option than yelling at him in frustration. Maybe she was normally a very sensitive mother but, as a result of what psychologists sometimes call "pile-up," she was dealing with emotional overload and her coping reservoir was depleted. Or, perhaps she simply did not understand the importance of recognizing and acknowledging her child's feelings.

Regardless of the reasons this mother treated her son as she did on that particular day, if their interaction was typical, there's reason for concern about their relationship and communication patterns during the years ahead. The adolescents I've interviewed didn't feel that conversations between them and their parents were substantive *or* sensitive in nature. I particularly remember one young man's summary: "They really almost never ask me how I'm doing. . . . [They say], 'If you need to say something, we're here.' But then they never are when I need to talk."

We all would readily agree that listening to children is a key ingredient to effective communication. Tiny infants are eager to let their parents know when they are hungry, tired, or experiencing some other source of discomfort. We as parents learn to read their verbal and non-verbal cues, anxiously attempting to determine what they are trying to "say" so we can respond in an appropriate fashion. If we feed a child who is sleepy rather than hungry, a communication breakdown has occurred. In the first months of our children's lives they are totally dependent on us to "listen" and understand. As they become toddlers and preschoolers they begin to add speech, one word or phrase at a time, to their mode of communication. With some exceptions, three-year-olds generally chat happily about anything and everything in their little worlds.

During the first few years of life, attentive and responsive listening establishes a pattern of welcoming child-parent communication. Openness invites further communication; conversely, being closed discourages our children from continuing (or maybe even starting) to speak. In addition to our words, our body language needs to convey "I'm listening; I want to understand; I care."

As an example, let's suppose that when it's time to get dressed for preschool a child says, "I don't want to go." An open response, consistent with listening for feelings as discussed above ("Can you tell me why you don't want to go to school?"), would attempt to determine the feelings behind the words. By contrast, closed responses tend to take control of the situation. These usually consist of giving commands ("It doesn't matter if you want to go; just hurry up and get dressed."), pretending there is no problem ("Of course you want to go. You love preschool."), or offering an expedient "solution" ("You'll be fine once you get there.").

Consistently responding to children in a closed manner sends the message that the adult is in charge and the child's thoughts and feelings are insignificant and unimportant. One teen told me, "I think [my parents] would hear what I was saying, but they could never level my view with their own. It would be like, 'Well, you know what, that's nice, but hey, this is what the deal is.' It always comes back to, 'This is what Mom and Dad say. And it's right because Mom and Dad say it. And that's the way it's going to be.'"

Clear communication becomes increasingly tough as children get older and discussion topics become more complex and potentially confrontational. Inviting communication from our children when they are young sets the stage for meaningful and healthy interaction during the teen years when more is at stake than whether the child wears a blue or white shirt to school. When asked if she talked with her parents when her life wasn't going well, a teen responded, "No, I'd usually ask my friends for advice whenever something bad happened. 'Cause I didn't want . . . an adult's advice!" Then she added, quietly and thoughtfully, "If I'd have had adult advice, I'd probably have done a lot better."

How do we rate ourselves on the critical matter of listening to our children? On a scale of 1–10, with 10 being perfect (for any of us not prone to the pitfalls of humanity), what scores would we give ourselves?

- Do we physically focus on our children by getting on their level?
- Do we make eye contact?
- Do we display open body language that invites communication?
- Do our facial expressions convey respect?
- Do we listen patiently?
- Do we block out potential distractions to concentrate on what our children are saying?
- Do we refrain from interrupting or rushing them when they are speaking?
- Do we attempt to look past our children's words and interpret the true meaning of what they are saying?
- Do we encourage children to express, rather than suppress, their thoughts?
- Do we listen with empathy when our children are troubled?
- Do we attempt to discover the root of children's behavior and statements rather than superficially addressing the symptoms?

Once again, in this whole business of parenting, we are faced with something that's much easier said than done. If we can give ourselves 6s, and maybe 7s, it means we're doing some things reasonably well. We just need to be consciously working toward 8s, 9s, and maybe even an occasional 10.

SENDING MESSAGES TO OUR CHILDREN

Above we quoted a portion of a Bible verse, "Everyone should be quick to listen."[6] The next phrase of that verse complements the first: "[Everyone should be] slow to speak."[7] The key to not speaking hastily is developing the practice of thinking first. (For some temperaments, this comes fairly easily. For others, it requires painstaking self-discipline, something I know from personal experience.) How many times have we said something thoughtlessly and wished we could take it back? Once they're spoken, taking words back is as difficult as putting toothpaste from the bristles of our toothbrush back into the tube.

Speaking too quickly seems to be a much more common occurrence than being too slow to reply. Pausing, taking a deep breath, saying a quick prayer for wisdom, and maybe even putting ourselves in a brief time-out helps us gain some perspective, whereas hasty retorts are emotionally rather than thoughtfully generated. I would like to think that as I have gotten older I've learned to be more reflective and less reactive, but being slow to speak is still far from second nature for me.

When interviewed by reporters, I know my words might appear in print or be heard on the airways the next day. I find myself choosing my words very carefully. I, as well as those with whom I communicate, would benefit from my routinely practicing such deliberate, thoughtful speech.

I suspect that very few of us could say with integrity that we always control our speech. Sadly, the ones we love the most generally bear the brunt of our thoughtless and disrespectful words. In a biblical passage that never ceases to bring me personal conviction, we read, "With the tongue we praise our Lord . . . and with it we curse human beings, who have been made in God's likeness. Out of the same mouth come praise and cursing. My brothers and sisters, this should not be."[8] And then the writer adds a piercing question: "Can both fresh water and salt water flow from the same spring?"[9]

We'd prefer that these cautions not apply to the way we speak to our children. After all, at some point even well-behaved children are annoying and disobedient; of course, they'll bring out the worst in us. The reality is that it is not okay to adopt a misguided double standard when it comes to our relationships with adults versus those with our children. We should no more scold a child for accidentally spilling milk on the kitchen floor than we would a friend for spilling coffee on the living room sofa.

Children should be expected to behave in a childish manner. We, on the other hand, should be held to a higher standard—both because we are adults and because our children are watching us. As the Apostle Paul says, "When I was a child, I talked like a child, I thought like a child, I reasoned like a child. When I became a man, I put the ways of childhood behind me."[10] One gauge of our maturity (or lack thereof) is the manner in which we talk to our children.

Another important principle when dealing with children's behavior is this: Whenever possible, messages should be given in the first person ("I") rather than the second ("you").[11] Admittedly, when we are frustrated or upset by another, the natural reaction is an accusation that begins with "you." But take a moment to contrast "What are *you* thinking—tromping in the house and getting mud all over the floor I just scrubbed!" and "*I* feel frustrated when the floor *I* just scrubbed gets all muddy." "You" messages tend to blame others while "I" messages express the speaker's thoughts and feelings. Generally, the former make our children defensive and resistant while the latter help them develop empathy as they become more aware of others' feelings. Although sending "I," rather than "you," messages isn't instinctive for most of us, it can be acquired through practice.

One final thought regarding sending messages to our children. Children, even at a very young age, can acquire a malady called "parent deafness." How often have we heard a parent command a child to do something and we absolutely knew that the child was not going to comply? The parent knew, too, and, out of habit, was prepared to repeat the message in an increasingly demanding manner, gradually adding threats, until the child at least acknowledged he was being addressed.

Many children don't obey initially because they've learned to predict the precise point at which parents actually mean what they are saying (e.g., when "Tommy" becomes "Thomas" and then "Thomas Edward"). Children are much more likely to obey if we follow the old adage to "say what we mean and mean what we say"— the first time.

Another key to minimizing children's parent deafness is to get the child's attention before we speak. Children, who are by nature fascinated, curious, and easily distracted, seldom tune in immediately to a parent's voice. We can save both our children and ourselves a great deal of frustration by making sure that we, rather than the tiny brown ants that are busily building a dwelling in the sidewalk cracks, have their attention. A good way to begin communication with a child is by making eye contact and asking, "Are you listening?"

A final suggestion regarding helping our children hear, understand, and respond is to follow our statements by a simple question: "What did I say?" This practice lessens the probability of miscommunication and enhances accountability. If a child repeats, "I need to pick up my toys and put them on the shelf before I can go outside to play," she is less likely to contend that she didn't hear or understand what she was expected to do.

Here are some questions that will serve as a self-check on sending messages to our children:

- Am I likely to speak hastily and wish I hadn't? Or do I remain quiet until I am composed and can respond in a thoughtful manner?

- Based on the way I speak to my children, would I be considered a mature or immature individual?
- When I am upset with my children, am I more likely to calmly send "I" messages ("I feel . . .") or angrily send "You" messages ("You always . . .")?
- Do my children have parent deafness? If so, why? What specific steps can I take to attempt to minimize it?
- Do I ask my children to repeat my words to make certain they have understood what I have said?

Perhaps the most important principle of communication really doesn't have to do with sending and receiving messages. Rather, it has to do with the state of our hearts. As we are reminded in the New Testament, "Out of the abundance [overflow] of the heart the mouth speaks."[12] And, just as we speak from our hearts, we listen with our hearts. Trying to change the way we listen and speak, without first changing our heart attitude, is quite futile.

Finally, assuming you are as human as I, don't be too disillusioned if you don't always communicate with your children the way you'd like to or know you should. Two little words, "I'm sorry," let our children know that sometimes we mess up too. By asking their forgiveness, we are modeling two additional character traits we'd like our children to possess: humility and a willingness to admit our mistakes.

Chapter 6
THE CHAIN OF COMMAND

Too many parents make life hard for their children by trying,
too zealously, to make it easy for them.
(JOHANN VON GOETHE)[1]

On a ship, the buck stops with its captain. In order for a vessel to successfully navigate and safely reach its intended destination, each crew member, whether first mate or ordinary seaman, must abide not only by the rules of the sea but also by the rules of his or her captain. The corresponding analogy to the family is obvious. Just as the captain must assume responsibility for the overall operations of a ship, so parents must maintain command of their family's ship. And, in all due respect to every great captain of the sea, I suspect that at times keeping a family on course makes guiding a ship seem relatively uncomplicated.

Of all topics that parents are anxious to discuss, discipline is consistently among the most common. Parents, weary of frustrating and exhausting daily hassles, want to be told specifically what to do when their two-year-old rubs applesauce into his hair and ears, carefully avoiding his mouth. The fact that this is considered normal toddler behavior is only minimally comforting to a parent who feels totally outmaneuvered by a 19-pounder in pull-ups.

So, how should we advise these parents? Relax, see the humorous side, and remember he'll grow out of this messy stage before you know it? Give him another helping of applesauce, assist him in holding his spoon, and praise any attempt to actually get the food in the vicinity of his mouth? Firmly but calmly explain to him that his behavior is unacceptable and a repeat performance will result in his not getting applesauce again until he learns to eat properly? Run to get the camera to preserve this moment for posterity? Immediately whisk him to the bathtub, scrub him down, and put him to bed? Ignore him and retreat to your own "happy place"? So many options, but how do we determine what is best for that particular parent-child duo on that particular day?

Many times each day, without the luxury of a trusted personal parenting consultant standing by, parents make decisions about if, how, and when to discipline their children. Interestingly, much discipline is based on a parent's current mood, circumstances, and level of stress as opposed to the child's behavior. If you are feeling relaxed, with time to recognize and appreciate your toddler's playful ingenuity, you might perceive the applesauce incident as an amusing photo op. On the other hand, if you simply must leave the house in ten minutes and you have yet to get a morning shower, patience and humor are difficult—if not impossible—to conjure up. Given the degree of variability within any household at any given moment, how does a parent maintain proper balance and "captain" status?

WHO'S IN CHARGE?

Through the years, others have referred to me as a child advocate and defender of youth. I am greatly disturbed when children are dishonored and disrespected, simply because they've had less time to mature and be socialized in a manner acceptable to the adults in their lives. Now let me deal with a related issue, which could be considered the flip side of the coin.

Treating children fairly and respectfully is one thing; allowing them to *control* the authority figures in their lives is quite another. At times, it seems that some of today's parents have confused the two. They seem to believe that it is okay for children to be in charge. (I question that a ship finds its way with an ordinary seaman at the helm.) Sometimes we as parents need a sign on the refrigerator that says, "I am the parent, s/he is the child," lest we forget. I sadly acknowledge that there seems to be some legitimacy in an observation by Edward VIII, Duke of Windsor, who said: "The thing that impresses me most about Americans is the way parents obey their children."[2]

Most homes can be characterized, to varying degrees, as either child-controlled or parent-controlled. In homes where the children are in charge, parents are frazzled and exhausted by their children's continual wants and demands. In-charge children, whose manipulative behaviors may include whining, nagging, belligerence and tantrums, have learned how to get their parents to obey. But children are not really to blame for this unfortunate role reversal; they have only taken control because their parents have relinquished it.

That's why there is so much frustration and tension in homes where children are fed whenever they say they're hungry but aren't required to eat reasonable amounts at mealtime; where they're allowed to skip naptime—no matter how tired and cranky—because they protest so vehemently; and where they're discontented unless they're being entertained by someone or some electronic form of media.

Although limited and appropriate child-choice teaches children to make responsible decisions, young children should not be given numerous options about anything. In amazement, I have observed parents allowing three-year-olds to pick out any pair of shoes they want, with literally dozens from which to choose. What kind of concept does a three-year-old have of function, practicality, comfort, or economy? Children simply aren't good at being in charge. Why?

There's no way they can possibly know what's best for them. As one writer says, "Wisdom comes only from experience—the big thing a child is short on."[3]

Distinguishing between child- and parent-controlled families isn't particularly tough for an outside observer. However, accurately evaluating one's own family can be quite difficult—particularly because no adult cares to admit to being manipulated by a child.

To attempt to evaluate who's in charge at your home, take a moment to answer the following questions with your family's daily routine in mind:

- Do your children procrastinate, argue, and question every-day instructions and rules? Do they commonly continue to nag after you have said "no"?
- Do you routinely engage in debate and compromise with your children, or give in to their demands?
- Do you tell your children certain consequences will occur but then not follow through?
- Do you frequently put your children's demands for attention above your own responsibilities and needs?
- When you go somewhere without your children, do you bring them a gift (or otherwise "compensate") because you didn't take them with you?
- Do you offer your child too many choices and allow him or her to make decisions that you should be making?

Around 18 to 24 months most toddlers begin to seriously "test the waters" in a quest to determine who's in charge. If you are expecting your first child, or your child is still an infant, now is the time to determine to have a home in which children obey their parents, rather than vice versa. Needless to say, this is much easier said than done.

There are several parental factors that make being in charge particularly difficult for some parents, including a meek, highly sensitive, or relaxed personality; a tendency to avoid conflict at all cost; an exaggerated desire to be "needed" as a parent; and current or past troubled relationships with one's own parents. Additionally, there are child characteristics, such as being strong-willed, and familial factors, such as divorce, that increase the likelihood children will control their parents. If any, some, or most of these characteristics describe your situation, you may be particularly vulnerable to being controlled by your children. I encourage you to take any necessary steps to avoid being caught in this trap, which is detrimental to you, your child, and the relationship between the two of you.

If you sense that you have relinquished the reins of control to your children, take heart. It's not too late to change. You can make a commitment right now to reclaim your rightful and essential place as authority in your child's life. It can be done, and there are several compelling reasons to do so. First, the Bible clearly instructs children to obey their parents: "Children, obey your parents . . . for this is right."[4] For families to function properly, that's the way it must be. When children disobey their parents, they are also disobeying a much higher power—God Himself.

Second, bear in mind that children who have too much decision-making power are less likely to mature well, especially in the areas of social and emotional development.

Third, parents who have a sense of control are less stressed and frustrated, and thus are better able to meet the genuine needs of their families.

Finally, as I have noted throughout this book, the patterns of control formed during early childhood will very likely carry over into the teen years, when the stakes are much higher than whether or not a child washes his hands before dinner.

You might be surprised to learn of a recurring theme among teens at a residential facility because of acting-out behaviors: Their parents should have been stricter. Some recall parents who gave them a lot of freedom, which, in turn, gave them lots of opportunities to mess up. Others say they got into trouble because their parents didn't enforce the rules.

We can safely assume that at the same time these teens were making poor choices regarding risky and antisocial behaviors, they were sending a plethora of decisive messages to their parents to discourage them from involvement in their children's lives. The teens' verbal as well as nonverbal communication likely indicated, "I want to be my own person," "I don't need you to tell me what to do," and "I don't care what you think."

And yet, in retrospect, they clearly wished their parents *had* taken control. This is still another reminder that parents need to be committed to optimum rules of parenting, based on sound principles, rather than the messages their children are sending.

THE ULTIMATE OBJECTIVE

Much like deciding our destination before we embark on a journey, we need to understand our purpose for discipline before determining appropriate guiding principles. Why do we discipline our children? First, let's attempt to understand what discipline is—and what it is not. Discipline comes from the root word "disciple," which is defined as "a convinced adherent of a school or individual."[5]

Discipline is all about training our children by passing along a belief structure of standards and morals whereby they can live. And, if nothing else stays with you after you've read this discussion of discipline, I hope you'll remember this one principle, which I believe to be foundational to all others: The ultimate objective of discipline is self-regulation.

The purpose of discipline is to teach our children to connect the dots between behavior and consequences, to be respectful and responsible, and ultimately to be prepared to function as adults in the real world. Do we get it? Discipline is training children so they no longer need external influences, such as parental instructions or demands, to do what is right; instead, an internal belief system kicks in to guide their thoughts and actions.

To take this one step further, a true disciple doesn't just blindly follow, but also believes in the mentor's doctrine. This brings us to another critical component of discipline: discretion. We as parents are not to pass along a hodgepodge of ideas that may or may not have merit. Rather, we are to transmit to our children the beliefs to which we adhere, in which we firmly believe.

The notion here is that we as parents have already sifted and sorted and come to conclusions about how life should be lived. When parents say they are not going to tell their children what to believe—that they want their children to "explore all options" (in matters such as moral values, lifestyle, and religion)—it appears that there is an absence of "discipline" in the true sense of the word.

In stark contrast to discipline, punishment is "suffering, pain, or loss that serves as retribution"; "severe, rough, or disastrous treatment."[6] Discipline is proactive and instructive and is directed at the behavior; punishment is reactive and punitive and is directed at the child.

As Charles Kingsley said, "There are two freedoms: the false where one is free to do what he likes, and the true where he is free to do what he ought."[7] The goal of discipline is self-regulation, which means that our children will grow up to do what they ought.

We all know that it is common for young children to balk when asked to comply with straightforward, everyday requests: pick up your toys, put on your shoes, come to the dinner table, get in the car. What, if any, guidelines can effectively and consistently direct spur-of-the-moment, as well as more pragmatic, decisions about discipline? The suggestions that follow pertain only partially to our children. For the most part, they have more to do with *our* attitudes and behaviors than those of our offspring.

One of the keys to effective discipline is that, rather than going along with the popular or trendy advice of the day, we make decisions based on the big picture—the people our children will someday become. This approach requires that our children understand there are both privileges and responsibilities inherent in being a part of the Smith, Jones, or Jackson family. Regardless of whether this status is viewed positively or negatively, it is a fact of life.

For our family, expectations placed on our children included living by the rules of the Mumford household. I still vividly remember the sight of our small son sitting dejectedly on the curb, slumped shoulders, elbows on his knees, and chin in the palms of his hands. His two same-age buddies were happily riding their tricycles in the street. He, on the other hand, was only allowed to ride in our driveway.

He could view this situation as nothing other than a travesty of justice. He was learning a painful truth at a very early age: Like it or not, at times there would be discrepancies between his rules and those of his friends. At the time of this incident, I had no concept of how relevant this principle would become during the "everybody's-doing-it" teenage years.

The decision regarding the big wheel episode was quite simple and straightforward for me: In my mind, a three-year-old riding in the street posed a serious threat to his physical well-being. End of story. Although I didn't like seeing him so unhappy, I wasn't at all inclined to change my mind. It was also relatively easy to enforce his staying out of the street because our son, who was tiny enough to find a curb-height seat quite comfortable, knew the momentary rush of disobedience wasn't worth the inevitable unpleasant consequences.

Additionally, he had not honed the skills of arguing persuasively, attempting to induce guilt by questioning my sense of fairness, or causing me to question my own judgment. You know where I'm going with this, don't you. Variations of the tricycle episode were repeated countless times as our son (and his younger brother) progressed through childhood and adolescence.

Unfortunately but predictably, as situations became more complex and convoluted I sometimes lacked my previous clear-cut conviction and confidence. But I would mentally revisit my first encounter with a parental decision at odds with those of other parents and attempt to employ the same criterion I did years earlier: what I believed to be best for our son. With that bottom line, it was much easier for me to fulfill my duties as a focused captain, rather than continually second-guess my decisions and meander all over the waterfront.

PARENTAL WARMTH AND CONTROL

As would be anticipated, research clearly indicates that parental style, including discipline and modeling, are predictors of behaviors. We've talked about treating children kindly and about parental versus child control. Let's now focus on the role and relationship of these two aspects of parenting. Perhaps you are familiar with a classic and time-tested categorization of parenting styles: permissive, authoritarian, and authoritative.[8]

A *permissive* (or "indulgent") parenting style is characterized by "child-control," as discussed previously, where children have a great deal of decision-making power and are encouraged to determine their own standards and regulate their own behaviors.

Authoritarian parenting, with its "because-I-said-so" mentality, is dictatorial in style. These parents do not offer explanations or understanding; children are expected to simply comply with parents' demands with unquestioning obedience.

Authoritative parents set standards and boundaries in the context of love. They exercise firm control but remain sensitive to children's individual needs and desires. Perhaps one of the most important traits of authoritative parents is that they look beyond immediate results (such as cessation of whining and their own much-needed peace and quiet) to their children's long-term well-being.

The jury is in regarding which style of parenting is optimal for healthy child, as well as subsequent adolescent, development. Research has resulted in a very impressive list of the benefits of authoritative parenting compared to permissive and authoritarian styles. Compared to their peers, adolescents of authoritative parents are more self-confident, socially adept, responsible, self-reliant, and creative; they achieve higher school grades; they are less anxious and depressed; they have high levels of moral reasoning; and, they are involved in fewer problem behaviors.[9]

I used an in-class activity in a couple of the undergraduate courses I taught that presented a parenting dilemma to the students. They were instructed to get into small groups, discuss the problem, and role-play three different responses, consistent with each of the parenting types discussed above. Time after time, the students concluded (without prompting) that the optimal approach—the authoritative one—is a lot of hard work. Much more thought and energy is required for cooperative, pragmatic discipline than for dictatorial or permissive parenting. In order to stay the course despite the time and energy required, we must continually keep our eyes focused on the purpose and prize: our children's present and future well-being.

A critical but often overlooked aspect of discipline is what occurs after disciplinary action has been taken. Assuming the crisis is past, both you and your child are relatively calm, and the child is old enough to verbalize her thoughts, this is an opportune time to ask her (a) why discipline occurred, (b) what will happen if her behavior is repeated, and (c) what she can do differently, given a similar set of circumstances, in the future.

Finally, regardless of the child's age or specificity of the context, discipline provides the parent with a made-to-order opportunity to exhibit unconditional love. Children of all ages need to know that, despite their actions, parental love is something of which they can always be certain.

As a self-check in the area of discipline, consider how you would handle these scenarios:

- Your two-year-old has just lost the privilege of playing with a favorite toy for the fourth time today. You are exasperated, disappointed, and feeling ineffective; exchanging your stay-at-home-parent status to become a server at a nearby restaurant is starting to look better and better.
- Your three-year-old son turns bedtime into a battle of the wills. Even though he stays in bed (once he's finally there), he yells from his room asking for a drink of water, saying he needs to go to the bathroom, and complaining that his room is too dark.
- Your four-year-old frequently refuses to eat the meals served to the rest of the family then complains about being hungry between meals.
- Your six-year-old son hit another child in the face with a soccer ball. You think it was an accident, but you're not sure.
- You attempt to monitor your seven-year-old daughter's homework each day after school. She routinely uses every excuse possible to get out of doing it, such as saying the work is too hard, complaining of a stomachache, saying she's tired, and saying the teacher doesn't care whether or not she does it.
- When you take your eight-year-old son shopping, he incessantly begs you to buy the latest toys or clothes for him.

Possibly your parenting style doesn't fit neatly into one of the three parenting approaches outlined above. Maybe you aren't sure how you'd respond to some of the above-described situations. That's certainly no cause for alarm. What matters, and what I'd like for you to remember from this discussion, is the importance of including two critical, complementary components as you discipline: *warmth* (being caring and responsive) and *control* (maintaining your role as an authority figure).

COMPOSURE

Previously we discussed parents who loudly reprimand and even swat their children in public. By exhibiting this type of behavior, they have failed to adhere to a very basic premise of effective discipline: parents being in control of their own words and actions.

Parents who do not restrain and control *themselves* are certainly not in a proper state of mind to positively influence their *children's* emotions and behaviors. When adults lose their composure, parent-child interaction is reduced to nothing more than that of two quarreling children.

Parents who struggle with self-control need to learn how to quickly and effectively manage their own actions before addressing those of their children. One helpful guideline is to remember that anything that buys additional time and allows you to think before you react (such as slowly counting to 20, saying a quick prayer, taking some deep breaths, or even putting yourself in "time-out") will increase the likelihood that you will discipline in a sensible manner.

When attempting to handle matters of discipline with composure, your goal is to respond in a calculated fashion, rather than to react emotionally and thoughtlessly. Firm decisiveness sets you apart as the one who is in control of not only the situation, but also of yourself. As children get older, they become more and more adept at spotting—and attempting to take advantage of—parental insecurities and vulnerabilities.

WISDOM

Perhaps you've heard the expression "Experience is learning from your own mistakes; wisdom is learning from someone else's." I like this principle, but I have to admit that I struggle with its application to the task of parenting. Because every child, every family, and every set of circumstances is so unique and complex, it seems that there are many things parents simply can't learn from someone else. Rather, as much as I hate to admit it, we are forced to rely on a certain degree of trial and error in matters of discipline and training. So it is this experimentation, of sorts, that leads to conclusions about what sometimes works with some children under some conditions—and what does not. Learning from our own successes and failures is perhaps the beginning of becoming wise parents.

On the topic of trial-and-error parenting, a dear friend with whom I shared many parenting joys and struggles quipped that our first children should be throwaways rather than real. She contended that we could practice and make all our mistakes on the first child and then move on to the actual child, feeling competent, relaxed and ready for whatever challenges were ahead. Unfortunately, even if it were feasible to have a trial run with a pretend child, what we learned would likely not apply to subsequent children, given the inevitable individual differences among offspring.

No doubt, parenting can be an intimidating task. Few parents would deny their sense of inadequacy when it comes to the matter of discipline. With our little one lying in the cradle, we would do well to echo Solomon's prayer when he was chosen as leader of the Israelites: "Give me wisdom and knowledge, that I may lead this people."[10]

We all need discernment to guide our children on the journey of life. And I know of nothing that drains our reservoir of ingenuity, tolerance, and judgment quicker than the matter of disciplining our children. I believe one reason it's so difficult is because they are *our* children—and we care so much.

"SAVE IT FOR THE BIGGIES"

There are a few rather simple phrases that helped guide my husband and me through years of decisions regarding discipline. One of those is "Save it for the biggies," or, phrased a bit differently, "This is not a hill to die on." Good advice, right? But even though I attempted to adhere to this principle, I quickly learned that it wasn't always easy to define a "biggie."

For one thing, what seems important at one age may seem totally inconsequential at another. Should my children be expected to make their beds each morning? The answer is probably "yes" if teaching my three-year-old daughter to be disciplined and responsible is high on my priority list. However, the answer may be "no," and an unmade bed seem quite trivial, when I realize that my 12-year-old has been lying to me about her math grade. So, does this mean that it is okay to expect my three-year-old to make her bed, but when she is 12 it no longer matters? Does that make any sense at all?

Another issue that complicates defining a "biggie" is that both a parent *and* a child are involved in any given situation, which means we are dealing with a myriad of personal variables. As an example, I continually battle the tendency to be a perfectionist—an attribute I suspect my family would describe as more than a tendency. When our sons were young, this translated into my expecting their rooms to be neat at all times. For one son this worked well. He, in fact, had built-in standards that made it difficult for him to go to sleep at night until everything was neatly in its place.

For the other son, his having an orderly room remained an elusive expectation; years of encouragement, training, and prodding generally turned out to be discouraging if not futile. With his laid-back and lighthearted spirit, he would readily respond to being asked to clean his room. Just as cheerfully, after the expenditure of what seemed to be substantial time and energy, he would call to me, "Time for an inspection." When I went to his room, I was consistently amazed that he actually thought that his room was "ready for inspection." He just didn't seem to be able to see things as I did—or as I thought he should. So, does this mean it's okay to have a certain set of standards for one child and a different set for another? What about consistency and fairness? Valid questions, for sure.

Here's how I put into practice the philosophy of "saving it for the biggies." I realized that if I attempted to address everything in our children's lives that didn't meet my standards, or of which I disapproved, by the time they were 12 my children would be totally parent deaf and I would be totally exhausted. I tried to distinguish between issues that were relatively insignificant and those that pertained to our child's character. My goal was to focus on the latter rather than the former.

Again, that little rule of thumb might sound good at face value. But you are no doubt astute enough to recognize that it's not exactly a panacea. If I tell my child that I expect him to keep his room orderly, and he leaves his clothes in piles on the floor, is that an inconsequential matter (one of housekeeping standards) or an issue of character (disobedience)? I truly wish the answers to these questions were more obvious.

Please pause for a second at this point to remember that I am committed to not giving simplistic solutions that may or may not work in the real world—or, in this case, with your real children. But I do trust that the principles and guidelines woven throughout these discussions will be helpful.

CHILDISH IRRESPONSIBILITY VS. WILLFUL DEFIANCE

Another guideline I have found extremely helpful in determining appropriate reactions is to attempt to determine the motives behind children's behaviors. A well-known psychologist says it like this: "Distinguish between willful defiance and childish irresponsibility. Forgetting, losing, and spilling things are not challenges to adult leadership."[11]

A child's *intention*, as best it can be deciphered, should dictate parental responses. As noted previously, children's and adults' behaviors shouldn't be expected to reflect the same level of maturity. Adults have a big advantage over children: They have had an opportunity to grow up. Forgetting to set the table and clumsily knocking food off the high chair tray are likely due to a child's cognitive or physical immaturity. Thus, these behaviors could rightfully be categorized as "childish irresponsibility."

By contrast, consider a child's refusal to set the table because it interrupts playtime or deliberately throwing food off the high chair tray as a means of demonstrating refusal to eat. These behaviors are obvious efforts to gain control by doing the opposite of what he has been asked or is expected to do. Thus, they can be interpreted as "willful defiance."

Determining a child's intention is an invaluable first step toward dealing with undesirable behavior. Childish irresponsibility requires understanding and patience. So does willful defiance. But, for the latter, the child must receive a clear and firm message: The behavior is not acceptable and must not continue.

BOUNDARY-SETTING

Much as buoys measure the appropriateness of water depth for seagoing vessels, boundaries give children parameters within which to operate. They help children distinguish between what is acceptable and unacceptable, appropriate and inappropriate, safe and unsafe, kind and unkind. A child needs to know that it is okay to accept a cookie from Grandma but not from a stranger on the playground. It is acceptable to express frustration by saying, "I want that toy," but not by pulling a playmate's hair to get it.

Boundaries are intended to keep toddlers from pulling lamps on their heads and teenagers from getting drunk. But how does a parent even begin to set appropriate and realistic boundaries? It can be a monumental task to protect our children not only from the big world out there, but, at times, from themselves.

For both brevity and clarity, I'd like to condense the discussion of boundaries to three steps: establish, communicate, and implement. Don't we all appreciate knowing what we can and cannot do? Doesn't a capable captain plainly spell out his or her expectations to the crew? Doesn't the crew understand the consequences of falling short of those expectations?

The first step, establishing boundaries, requires that parents consider what is appropriate, realistic, and fair for each child. Should a five-year-old be expected to come in for dinner at 6:00 without a reminder? Can we expect him to take responsibility without adult intervention? If so, we need to make certain he has a means to do so, such as an alarm on his wristwatch. So, if a wristwatch alarm works perfectly to get one five-year-old to dinner without a hassle, will it work for all five-year-olds? No—probably not, even for siblings.

Early childhood educators wisely make a distinction between *age* and *individual* appropriateness. Although guidelines based on age are helpful, individual differences make it unrealistic to have the same expectations for all children of a particular chronological age. In order to be consistently effective, even a procedure as seemingly simple as coming to dinner needs to be tailored to a child's individual temperament and abilities.

Once boundaries are established, they must be clearly communicated. The principles of sending and receiving messages, discussed earlier, can help parents make certain they and their children have the same expectations. Should the alarm be set for 5:55, allowing the child five minutes to come inside? Is he to be inside the back door or at the table with his hands washed by 6:00? Is it 6:00 according to his Superman wristwatch or according to the kitchen clock? Or, in keeping with the "save-it-for-the-biggies" philosophy, does whether or not he gets to dinner "on time" really matter at all?

You are in the best position to decide what is most appropriate and effective for your child. As you contemplate this, remember that boundaries aren't primarily about dinnertime, as important as it is. Rather, they are about training a child—to listen, to follow instructions, and to assume responsibility for her own actions. Although extreme rigidity is not advisable, on the other side of the coin, ambiguity and vacillation undermine the impact and purpose of boundary-setting. And some children are particularly adept at finding and using loopholes to their advantage.

The final facet of boundaries is follow-up. When a child comes in from outside on his own and is at the dinner table at 6:00, positive reinforcement is a useful tool for encouraging the child to repeat the desired behavior the next evening. This can be as simple as, "Good job getting to dinner on time," or "Mealtime is nicer for all of us when you come to dinner with no hassle."

On the other hand, when the child steps outside the parameters of the boundaries that were established and communicated, it is time for consequences. Notice the use of the word "consequences" as opposed to punishment. Consequences are administered in a respectful manner; they are for poor choices, not naughty children.

A tactic I think is very important is this: Whenever possible, parents should determine and convey consequences at the same time the boundaries are being established. The ramifications of this approach and its potential for simplifying the implementation of consequences are huge. If a child decides to be late for dinner, he has chosen to be subjected to the predetermined consequences, which should then come as no surprise. In a rather simple application of the cause-and-effect principle, the child—not the parent—has made the choice.

Parents repeatedly tend to fall back on the same discipline techniques—time-out, sending a child to his room, grounding. Although these definitely are suitable and sometimes produce the intended results, there are many occasions when more creative and unique discipline is likely to be more effective. Commonly advocated in parenting programs,[12] a "logical consequence" is fitted to the child's behavior. When logical consequences unfold, the child is more likely to connect the cause (his behavior) and the effect (the consequence he experiences).

If a child does not come in for dinner on time, a logical consequence is that the family eats without him. Note that in order to determine an effective consequence, you must know your child and what matters to him. If he doesn't care if the family eats without him, that consequence would certainly not serve its intended purpose. It might even give him a feeling of power and independence.

Another reminder is to make sure that you can live with the discipline you've decided to use. Setting consequences in advance, rather than at the time the offense occurs, lessens the likelihood you will impose discipline you might later regret. Regardless of whether it is predetermined or decided at the moment, once a child has been told the consequence of a certain behavior, it is generally undesirable to change it. But there are exceptions to that as well.

I recall a parent of a preschooler calling me one day in a rather frantic state. The previous evening she had told her son that he could not have anything else to eat until he finished his dinner. The tiny guy, less than one-fourth the size of his mother, seemed all too eager to engage in a battle of the wills; unfortunately for the parent, winning seemed to be a higher priority to him than eating. When the mother called me, many hours after his initial refusal, she could not stand the thought of his going another minute without at least a small bite of food. But she was also concerned about the future ramifications of "giving in" to him. How had she gotten into this predicament? The consequence was logical, wasn't it? All he had to do was finish his dinner. She never imagined a clash of epic proportions would ensue. One lesson here is that children, especially the determined variety, should never be underestimated.

How do parents avoid this sort of quandary? I suggest never using essentials, such as food, as bargaining chips. However, if you do find yourself facing a lose-lose situation like the one just described, try to put it in the perspective of the big picture. This is one relatively minor, albeit seemingly unsalvageable, incident and it does not mean you've failed as a parent.

I believe when it becomes clear that your child, rather than you, has assumed a dominant position in a battle of the wills, it is best to simply say, "I have changed my mind. Instead of your not getting anything else to eat until you have eaten what's on your plate, I have decided that you will not be allowed to . . ." Although the child shrewdly took control and avoided one particular consequence, he is faced with another one that, hopefully, the parent will be able to enforce.

Both in establishing and enforcing boundaries, as children get older, "fairness" becomes an increasingly bigger issue. A simple rule is to be certain we are not asking something of our children with which they *cannot*, rather than *will not*, comply. Realistic expectations are a must if we want to avoid resentment regarding the parent-child power differential and/or absolute refusal to obey.

Besides being realistic, another way to minimize protests of "it's not fair" is to have our children involved in establishing boundaries and determining the consequences of overstepping them. Scheduled, as well as impromptu, family meetings, which will be discussed in more detail in a few pages, can serve as a forum for developing and documenting family rules.

Needless to say, no matter how thoughtful and painstaking our approach to discipline, there will be times when we are caught off guard and are struggling with whether the boundaries and their consequences are equitable. Asking our children what they think is a legitimate approach. But, lest we regard getting their input as a panacea, let me share with you just a couple of instances when our sons and I disagreed about boundaries and I elicited help from them.

I remember when one of our sons was telling me that I was being unfair to not let him go somewhere with his friends. At that point

I apparently was feeling I wasn't on very solid ground, and I wasn't sure how to respond. Wanting him to consider it from my perspective and give me his input, I said, "Let's reverse roles. I'm the child. I think you're being unfair not to let me go." Much to my surprise and dismay, he responded, "But I said it's *fine* if you go."

Just to let you know that not just one but both of our sons were capable of outsmarting me, I also recall trying to reverse roles with the other son on a matter related to discipline. I asked him, "What would you do if you were the parent and I was the child?" Without a second's hesitation, he answered, "I'd ask you what you would do if you were the parent and I was the child." So much for getting help from them!

MONITORING

Where does monitoring enter the picture? When children are little, monitoring means making sure they don't put their fingers into electrical outlets or chase a ball into the street. When they're elementary age, we make certain they are ready for their spelling quiz and they actually turn off their bedroom lights somewhere near the agreed-upon time. Beyond the specifics, though, monitoring is conveying the sense to our children that there's someone to whom they answer and there is someone who cares whether or not they comply with the family's standards. Children who are not mature enough to consistently monitor their own behaviors need assistance to do so. As adults, we refer to this concept as accountability.

Once again, as children get older the stakes become higher. Rather than a matter of their being tired at school because they turned the light off at 8:27 instead of 8:00, ignoring a midnight curfew could lead to late-night opportunities to get into serious trouble. Research has repeatedly shown that parental monitoring is protective because it makes teens less likely to be influenced by peers and make poor choices such as abusing substances.[13]

Now for some final remarks regarding discipline. A pattern that I've seen played out many times is the tendency for parents to be caught off guard when their children become 11, 12, or 13 and start making choices and displaying behaviors contrary to what they have been taught. In defense of parents, it really is quite disconcerting when the behavior of an obedient and loving child changes suddenly and dramatically.

For instance, when a 12-year-old would rather hang out at the mall on Friday evening than participate in the family's movie and popcorn ritual, dismay and concern are predictable parental responses. Remember that this is the time for logic and reason ("our little girl is growing up"), rather than overreaction ("our daughter hates her family"). I must quickly add that the latter is an understandable response to entering uncharted and seemingly unfriendly waters.

In case my repeatedly mentioning the challenges of adolescence has you feeling increasingly uneasy, let me digress briefly at this point to assure you that adolescence and disaster are not synonymous terms. Although some teenagers exhibit rather severe acting-out behaviors, the vast majority navigate the teen years without major trauma. To say adolescence is relatively problem-free, however, is not to suggest that it is uneventful. Every "normal" adolescent is affected by the combination of physical, social, emotional, and cognitive changes that are inherent at this developmental stage. These changes promote autonomy and independence, necessary components of maturation. They also necessitate changes in family relationships and interaction.

When children believe parents are overreacting, the parent-child relationship, as well as the specific issue (such as missing curfew), tends to deteriorate rather than improve. To illustrate, when I asked troubled teens about discipline, a consistent lament was that their rules became stricter as they became older. They felt that when they wanted to be *more* independent their parents tightened the reins. Based on the teens' remarks, there was an unquestionable pattern of their rules becoming stricter as their externalizing behaviors increased. Many of these teens responded to stricter rules with obstinacy and disobedience.

So, what's a parent to do? Surely they can't be faulted for stiffening the rules as their child's behavior deteriorates. Once again, simple solutions don't exist. But we do know that parents need to set the pattern early and continue to discipline their children with composure, warmth, and firmness.

Both the parent and child need to understand that (a) the rules and expectations will likely be adjusted (whether they become more or less lenient) as children's behaviors change; and (b) the parent remains the ultimate authority until children become self-sufficient and independent of the family in which they were raised.

Remember the principle of promoting self-regulation? Discipline isn't just about calming today's turbulent waters and avoiding icebergs. It's attempting to ensure that our children are eventually capable of steering their own boat.

FAMILY MEETINGS

Previously we discussed various parenting styles. The authoritarian approach, which is heavy on control with little warmth, tends to result in belligerence, dependency, and insecurity. One of the missing components in this approach is communication. "Because I said so" is deemed by the parent as a sufficient reason to enforce rules; no explanation is offered or considered necessary. The problem with this approach isn't so much that parents are making the decisions; that's generally as it should be. However, when parents are seen as unyielding and insensitive autocrats, they are inviting their children to question, protest, and even rebel.

Family meetings are a way to promote communication, understanding, and a sense of respect among family members. Simply put, they are an opportunity for each family member to listen and to be heard on any topic he or she believes to be important. These family times can include fun topics (e.g., deciding where the family will go for Sunday's picnic), practical issues (e.g., who's taking Sara to gymnastics tomorrow), as well as ample time to discuss, establish and revisit the set of rules by which the family lives.

Obviously, meetings need to be designed to fit each individual family and the content needs to be altered as children get older and family needs and dynamics change. A child of three may have little to contribute but at 13 may have a whole lot to say. But the basic rules that govern these family times can remain fairly simple and consistent. For example, (a) all family members will be present; (b) anything can be shared, as long as it is stated in a respectful and appropriate manner; (c) each person has a right to speak without interruption or ridicule; (d) each person's input will be considered and valued; and (e) with everyone's opinions and needs carefully and sensitively weighed, the ultimate decision rests with the parent(s).

I've presented the concept of family meetings in a very simplistic way. But, rather than offering a precise blueprint, my purpose is to motivate you to consider initiating regular family meetings in your home. If suited to your family dynamics, individual temperaments, and diverse needs, this forum can play a valuable role in promoting healthy interaction and connectedness. Additionally, you are establishing a potentially meaningful and useful precedent as your family grows and changes.

The following checklist may guide you as you attempt to evaluate your discipline practices:

- When disciplining my child, does my discipline more accurately reflect my child's actual behavior that I am attempting to correct or my own mood, circumstances or stress level?
- When disciplining my child, do I consider the "big picture"— the person my child will someday become—rather than short-term convenience or ease?

- When committed to a particular ideology because I believe it to be best for my child, do I waver based on what other parents allow their children to do?

- Do I really believe that discipline is *good* for my child? If so, do my words and behaviors demonstrate this belief?

- Do I allow my child to control our household by acquiescing to his/her continual wants and demands? (Because it is so difficult for us to see ourselves as we really are, perhaps a trusted friend can help you answer this question.)

- Is my discipline characterized by a balanced combination of warmth and control? If not, do I feel it should be?

- Do I maintain my composure rather than disciplining my child in anger?

- Do I get "hung up" on relatively insignificant behaviors, or do I attempt to distinguish the truly important from the relatively unimportant?

- Do my discipline strategies suggest I understand the difference between childish irresponsibility and willful defiance?

- Am I training my child to listen, follow instructions, and assume responsibility for her behaviors?

A ship safely reaches its intended destination under the watchful eye of its captain, who must make certain all crew members understand and abide by the rules of the sea. The captain knows well what is required for safe navigation and realizes that poor decisions—on the part of any one of the ship's crew—can lead to calamity. The crew may not always appreciate the standards to which they are expected to adhere. Nevertheless, a good captain undauntedly stays the course. Are you, as captain of your family's ship, providing the calm, firm and goal-oriented direction that your children need?

Chapter 7
A TRUSTWORTHY COMPASS

We cannot direct the wind, but we can adjust the sails.
(BERTHA W. CALLOWAY)[1]

In an oft-quoted Scripture verse, the writer of Proverbs urges parents to "train up a child in the way he should go."[2] The words "train up" suggest to me that there is more to raising children than the laissez-faire belief that babies arrive on the scene preprogrammed and, thus, parents should simply stay out of the way and "let nature take its course." This hands-off approach stresses heredity over any environmental influences; therefore, parents are only accountable for their child's behaviors to the degree that they are responsible for their genetic make-up.

Adherence to this viewpoint relieves parents of any liability should things go wrong or, for that matter, any credit should things go right. In fact, the laissez-faire philosophy makes a book such as this totally unnecessary. But I believe that leaving our children's training to chance is no less absurd than attempting to navigate without a trustworthy compass or allowing the wind to carry us at will.

If you're still reading, I assume you give at least partial mental assent to the above-quoted proverb about training. "Training a child in the way he should go" is consistent with setting goals for our children and making plans to achieve them, as discussed earlier. However, to complement the planning that's done in advance, we as parents also need to make the most of opportunities along the way.

TEACHABLE MOMENTS

Daily shared parent-child activities and routine chores provide innumerable teaching opportunities. These moments occur naturally, assuming two components are present: (a) the parent and child are together, and (b) the parent is tuned in to the child's world. The first point regarding togetherness is obvious, I know. But it's an important reminder that we cannot possibly take advantage of teachable moments, which by their very nature are spontaneous, when we are not with our children.

The second point, being tuned in to our children, has the potential of turning any time with our children into an invaluable opportunity. A teachable moment may present itself at the shopping mall, when a child spies an action figure he desperately wants. He can't buy it because he spent all his money last week on the impulsive purchase of a fancy-looking but cheaply made toy truck that is already in the trash.

A parent who responds to the child's plea with a patient, logical, and gentle explanation assists the child in making the connection between his past actions and current dilemma and is taking advantage of a teachable moment. By contrast, a parent who appeases him by giving him money to purchase the action figure is not.

RESPONSIBILITY

"With privilege, goes responsibility" is a phrase I remember using often when our children were young. Without much stretch of the imagination, I'm sure you can think of many fitting occasions to pass along this friendly reminder to your offspring. Not only do children need to understand the concept of giving as well as receiving; they need to have opportunities and experiences that will encourage them to become responsible.

Parents can fall into several different categories in this particular aspect of training. Some parents, possibly those who feel they were robbed of their own childhood by too much responsibility too soon, want to shield their own children from any potential "unpleasantness," including effort and self-discipline that accompany productivity. These parents allow their children to do only what they choose to do.

Other parents find it's much easier to simply do what needs to be done themselves rather than face the hassle of prodding resistant children. Still others fail to see the value of purposely teaching children to be responsible. Once again, as we consider the most effective way to parent, let's step back and look at the big picture: the people our children will someday become.

A four-year-old can easily be taught how to set the dinner table. If he willingly agrees that this will be his contribution to dinner ("with privilege, goes responsibility"—he plans to eat), initially it is likely to be fun for him and endearing to the parent—to say nothing of how pleased Grandma will be when she comes to visit.

But the first few days, before the novelty wears off, are only the precursor to actual training. Training begins when it's no longer a game that the child plays only if he's so inclined. When the child refuses to willingly assume the responsibility of regularly setting the table, we as parents are faced with a choice. We set the table ourselves, enlist someone else who will willingly oblige, or insist that he do it. The first two choices are much simpler in the short-term. However, in keeping with our commitment to look beyond the moment and think long-term, the third choice, in spite of its potential for discord and frustration, is a far superior option. Not insisting that children fulfill their responsibilities is an open invitation to rebel against future parental injunctions.

A few very simple guidelines can help us in our efforts to train our children to be responsible. First, our expectations must be realistic, that is, suited to our children's still-developing cognitive and fine motor skills. No amount of instruction can equip young children to safely handle the antique fruit bowl that has been in the family for five generations. But they are very capable of putting out the placemats and napkins.

Remember that training is a process that takes time and effort. Rather than assuming our children can read our minds, we need to explicitly explain and/or demonstrate—maybe several times—what we expect them to do and how they are to do it. If we give our children hurried, non-specific instructions (e.g., "set the table"), it is likely that our expectations will not be met. Worse yet, if we then admonish our children for not doing it "correctly," and proceed to rearrange the flatware or refold the napkins, we are sending the message that their efforts are inferior. Needless to say, this will affect how the child views future attempts to set the table.

Another guideline in effectively training our children and enhancing their perception of work is giving them choices whenever possible and as appropriate. If their responsibility is to assist in setting the dinner table, they can choose to either put out the plates and glasses or the spoons and forks. This will give them a sense of empowerment and the intended purpose is still achieved: They are being taught responsibility.

The final rule of thumb that minimizes potential distress, particularly for the parent, pertains to the outcome of the task children are asked to do. In the spirit of fostering creativity, we may want to give children some latitude regarding how the table is set. This is a good idea, assuming we can live with their decision to replace the freshly cut floral centerpiece with an array of toy soldiers or a dead bug collection.

SERVING OTHERS

The purpose of this brief section is to remind us of something I believe to be an essential and frequently overlooked component of child training: teaching our children to serve. Whether we like it or not, our children are growing up in an "it's-all-about-me" world. To counteract countless alluring invitations for self-gratification, and an "I-am-the-center-of-the-universe" mentality, we must conscientiously identify opportunities for our children to serve rather than to be served. This requires one commodity of which parents never seem to have enough: *time*.

But in order for our children to grow up to be sensitive to the cares and needs of others and to truly understand what it means to put others before themselves, opportunities for them to serve should be deliberately planned. We teach them the spirit and joy of serving not only by modeling it in our own lives (e.g., by caring for the neighbor's children so the exhausted mother can get a much-needed break from the daily routine) but also by directly involving them in service (e.g., by making small gifts for the residents of a local nursing facility and personally delivering them). By conscientiously incorporating service to others into your family's busy routine, you will be undermining society's message and human nature's tendency to focus on me and mine.

RESPECT

Previously, we discussed parents' treating their children with a lack of respect. Now, in the context of discipline, we will move on to a complementary phenomenon. In the past couple of decades I have observed a huge tendency for children, particularly when they reach pre-adolescent age, to treat their parents (and other adults) with disrespect. Is there a connection between the way children are treated by adults and the way they treat adults? No doubt. But

I speculate that parents' treating their children disrespectfully is only part of the problem. I believe that today's parents often fail to command respect as they should.

Command respect? That seems harsh for the 21st century, doesn't it? After all, unlike previous generations, we are attuned to "child rights" and the importance of parenting with sensitivity, warmth and compassion. But I use the term "command" advisedly and with conviction. Whatever the reasons, I believe parents have become increasingly unable or unwilling to establish positions of authority in their children's lives. Children learn to use nagging and whining effectively, and exhausted parents give in just to get some peace and quiet. Manipulative and coercive behaviors that are reinforced by parental compliance become powerful tools in an adolescent's arsenal.

The increased tendency for children to disregard authority figures extends beyond the home and affects other contexts, such as the school, as well. Over the years that I attended our sons' junior high open houses and sat in on their classes, I saw a pattern of deterioration of students' respect for their teachers, exhibited by talking without permission, interrupting, and a general disregard for the teacher's efforts to control what was going on in the classroom. Frankly, I was quite appalled by the students' apparent ability and eagerness to take advantage of weak and thus ineffective classroom management. Rather than its intended purpose, the classroom was providing opportunities for youth to hone the skills of exploitation, rudeness, and disrespect.

My increasing concerns regarding children's attitudes toward authority figures were reinforced and confirmed as I talked with troubled teens. One of the teen's attitudes was reflective of many: "I wanted to do what I wanted to do. And so I didn't want someone telling me that I couldn't do something." Several of the teens expressed disrespect not only for their parents but also for other authority figures, particularly those associated with law enforcement.

Very few children joyfully submit to authority since doing so seems to run counter to human nature. Nevertheless, orderly, well-balanced, and productive lives are not feasible in its absence.

MORALS AND BELIEFS

As has been evident throughout this book, my beliefs are based on the tenets of the Christian faith. An underlying conviction for all training in our home was that each of us is born with a "God-shaped vacuum," as Blaise Pascal, a 17th-century French philosopher, called it. John 3:16 states, "For God so loved the world that he gave his one and only Son, that whoever believes in him shall not perish but have eternal life."[3] We taught our sons that believing in Jesus for eternal life would fill that vacuum and following Him was a personal commitment—one that we could not make for them. This belief was foundational to all other training on spiritual matters.

Parents, the Bible says that it is our task to pass our faith along to our children. Note the following verse: "[God] commanded our ancestors to teach their children, so the next generation would . . . put their trust in God and would not forget his deeds but would keep his commands."[4]

Children can be taught from a very early age that the Bible is more than just another storybook. They can have a Bible of their own, with text and pictures appropriate for their age. Because it provides a guide for life, the Bible's authority and usefulness for instruction can very naturally be incorporated into daily living. When our elementary-aged children struggled with integrity, rather than just telling them that lying was wrong we'd ask them to get their Bible. Then we would help them find Exodus 20:16 and have them read what God had to say on the topic of lying: "You must not lie."

This wasn't in any way meant to be a heavy-handed tactic to "put the fear of God" into our children, making Him look like an oppressive dictator waiting to pounce when His subjects disappoint

Him. Rather, it was intended to help them understand that there's a reliable, clearly outlined guide to help them distinguish right from wrong whether or not we are around to remind them. We also hoped to impress our children with the desirability of looking to the highest and ultimate authority as a source of direction, comfort, and meaning.

Beyond the Bible itself, there are many Christian books that can have powerful and far-reaching impact on young children's lives. A favorite at our house, and a bedtime ritual for many years, was the ever-popular allegory, *The Chronicles of Narnia*.[5] My husband read the complete *Chronicles of Narnia* to the children several times before they began reading them on their own. I might add that both of our grown sons have read them with their children.

In addition to books, music can play a very powerful role in training young children. Our sons learned many, many Bible stories and biblical principles through the medium of music. Once, when our then-three-year-old son was listening to music in his room, a song began playing that he recognized. He called to me: "Mommy, I hear a song we sing at church. I wuv it; I just wuv it."

To this day, lyrics from songs to which my children listened when they were very young frequently come to mind and I find them not just nostalgic, but instructive. Music was an important part of our sons' childhood that we all shared. How could we miss the point of lyrics like, "Be patient, be patient, don't be in such a hurry. If you are impatient, you only start to worry,"[6] and "Kids under construction; maybe the paint is still wet. Kids under construction; the Lord may not be finished yet."[7]

I believe that Christianity is a way of life prompted by personal conviction, not simply a set of rituals by which we must abide. That being said, in addition to the practices mentioned above, there are many natural outgrowths of Christian beliefs that involve customs and routines—rituals, if you will. High on the list of importance in my mind is prayer. We can pray for our children when they are still in the womb, once they're in our arms, at the side of their cradles, and then by their cribs. We can pray not only for them, but also with them, as they grow older. If prayer is a natural, instinctual part of our lives, it is likely to become a part of theirs as well.

Prayer, no matter how simplistic its delivery, is talking with God. Through young children's mealtime prayers, they are learning to be grateful to God for providing their basic needs. When they tell God they're sorry for hitting someone, they begin to understand the concept of a forgiving God who cares about their choices and actions. And, when they ask God to help them not to be afraid of the dark, they begin to see Him as a source of protection and comfort.

Attending church is another ritual that our children learn from us. I have frequently observed families for whom sports, sleeping in, and even "family time," take precedence over going to church. I am not saying that occasionally missing church is inexcusable. But I do want to gently remind you that when other things consistently take priority over going to church or church-related activities, we are sending a clear message to our children about church's relative unimportance.

One reason I feel it is important to establish the churchgoing pattern early is because of what I've observed during many years as a youth group sponsor. When young children become adolescents and parents become increasingly aware of potentially negative peer influences, they often look to the church youth program for help. But, if church attendance hasn't been a priority up to this point, the child continues to view it as optional, and parents have little leverage for convincing their child otherwise.

One final note before we leave the topic of church attendance. This actually probably goes without saying, but I will make no assumptions here. Your young children should never, ever hear you grumble about the length of the sermon, the type of music, or anything else related to the pastors, the church, or its attendees. By succumbing to the temptation to voice dissatisfaction, parents seriously undermine the very principles they should be modeling.

We've talked throughout about the critical importance of modeling the behaviors we desire for our children. As a well-known child psychologist states, "Values are caught, not taught."[8] The sense of this statement seems to parallel the familiar adage attributed to Ralph Waldo Emerson: "What you do speaks so loud I can't hear what you're saying." Talking to our children about moral standards, and their underlying belief system, is relatively worthless if our words and behaviors communicate a message to the contrary. The ideal, then, is combining a consistent message of verbal teaching with modeling.

As you attempt to train your children in the way they should go, the following self-check may help guide you.

- Do I spend ample time with my children to take advantage of teachable moments?
- Do I frequently miss teachable moments because I'm engrossed in my own concerns and agenda rather than tuned in to my children's world?
- Are my expectations of my children realistic?
- Do I provide my children with opportunities to become responsible, or do I tend to spare them from things that aren't easy or fun?
- Are my children respectful of me and other adults?
- Do my behaviors indicate that I believe reading the Bible and praying are important?
- Do I model positive behaviors toward the church and my fellow parishioners, including regular attendance and no gossip or negative comments?
- Do I consistently teach and model the values by which I expect my children to live?

A captain depends on buoys to warn of potential danger and mark the path his ship can safely navigate. Similarly, the beliefs and values parents pass along to their children serve to guide them through unknown and dangerous waters and keep them headed in the right direction.

Chapter 8
CREATING A SAFE HARBOR

No culture has ever been able to provide a better shipyard for building storm-proof vessels for the journey of man from the cradle to the grave than the individual nourished in a loving family.
(LAURENS VAN DER POST & JANE TAYLOR)[1]

*O*ur 13-year-old son rushed in the back door, took a deep breath, and exclaimed, "I'm so glad to be here. It's like rounding third base and heading toward home. I know I'm finally going to be safe." The school bus ride had been particularly unsettling for a sensitive young man. Two older students in the back of the bus were unabashedly offering drugs to their peers and our son's sense of security was shaken. He had run as fast as he could from the bus stop to our back door and arrived breathlessly. I was waiting with a hug, a snack, and a listening ear. He had reached a safe harbor.

One of the greatest gifts we can give our children is a sanctuary—a place of security and protection. Much as God is "a shield to all who take refuge in Him,"[2] our responsibility as parents is to provide security for our children who look to us for refuge. Anthropologist Margaret Mead is quoted as saying, "One of the oldest human needs is having someone wonder where you are when you don't come home at night."[3] Inherent in this statement is the sense that someone truly cares for you.

Research findings consistently indicate that a sheltering home environment enhances children's early development. It also lessens the probability that when they reach the adolescent years, they will make poor decisions regarding behaviors such as alcohol and drug use.[4]

I was struck by the apparent absence of a haven for many teens at the residential facility because of their own inappropriate behaviors and the ensuing family conflict. They appeared sad as they expressed their perceptions of their families and homes. One told me that she had felt isolated and described herself as "looking for someone to go to when I had problems . . . someone who'd care about me and care what would happen to me." Another's comments were equally poignant: "I knew that I didn't have anyone in the world." Linked to the teens' perceived lack of support and love was a search to find someone—anyone—to fill that void.

The time to cultivate an atmosphere that will continue to draw your children in, rather than push them away, is while they are young. Take a moment to reflect on these questions. What is it like, through a child's eyes of innocence and dependence, to be a part of your family? Have you taken time to carefully evaluate your home and ensure that what happens there is not left to chance? Let's discuss a few specific components of the home environment that affect children's sense of self, belonging, and security.

TRAVELING AT HOW MANY KNOTS?

If your home is commonly characterized by what might be described as "rush hour," think for a moment about what your children might say if they could identify and articulate their feelings. Would it possibly be something like: "Why don't I ever have time to see if I can make some words from my alphabet cereal?" "Why do you always say 'hurry, hurry, hurry'?" "Can I just have some time to play?"

Rushing is contrary to children's nature. Although adults sometimes assume children have limitless adaptability, they are actually very susceptible to stress. Children often fail to respond during a barrage of parental commands like, "Get your shoes on NOW!" and "If you don't come NOW, I'm going to leave without you!" (an inappropriate as well as empty threat). Why? They are attempting to gain some control over circumstances that go against the core of their beings.

I often remind parents that attempting to rush preschoolers by telling them they're going to be late is a total exercise in futility. As we know, preschoolers' thinking is characterized by self-absorption. Practically, this means that nothing starts until they have arrived; therefore, it is not possible for them to "be late."

Hurrying has permeated many aspects of today's family life. In part, the current trend to register young children in activities—ballet, gymnastics, T-ball, piano—is responsible for the unfortunate combination of snack foods and catnaps in the back seat of an SUV.

Sooner is not necessarily better when it comes to enrolling children in structured activities. Particularly poor choices are activities that do not suit a child's schedule or inflict pressure to achieve beyond his capabilities. By contrast, parent-child picnics at the park, trips to the library, baking and delivering cookies to a housebound elderly friend, and playing soccer in the backyard can be arranged around the family schedule, enjoyed at a leisurely pace, and individually suited to children's aptitude, interests and stamina.

A notable phrase among persons in the field of child development is "Play is a child's work." Optimum development unfolds naturally in the context of a carefree, stimulating environment that encourages exploration, choice, initiating, creating, exercising, imagining—simply being a child. Free play in small, informal groups provides opportunities for interaction, cooperation, sharing, and communication under a parent's watchful eye and establishes the foundation for the formation of future relationships.

On a related point, we put much emphasis on early social inter-action and adult-initiated cognitive stimulation, and rightly so. But rarely do we discuss the importance of young children being allowed solitary time. When a seven-month-old is observing the cause and effect of grasping and shaking a chain of colorful plastic letters, we do not need to always "seize the moment" to talk about colors and the letters of the alphabet.

When a toddler is happily engaged with building nothing in particular out of blocks, it is not necessary that we intervene at that moment to demonstrate how to build a house or a barn. When a seven-year-old is constructing a "science experiment" out of straws, sand, rubber bands, and discarded whipped topping containers, we do not need to interrupt his thoughts to interject our good ideas.

As an aside, think about whether it's sometimes possible that when parents force their way into their children's world it's a reflec-tion of their own, rather than their child's, needs. I think so. A mother who needs to feel needed, or a father who equates being alone with loneliness, is much less likely to allow a child time to experience the wonder of independent exploration and discovery.

Young children's abilities are being stretched as they examine, contemplate, and manipulate on their own. And it's so important to remember that whether a young child is experimenting with black and purple finger paint or making snowmen out of marshmallows, *the process is more important than the product*. Through solitary play, young children learn to think, function, and make independent deci-sions. They also learn that being alone can be more than tolerable or acceptable; it can be fun. Even being "bored" is not the end of the world and does not require adult intervention.

Why do I feel this is noteworthy? Early patterns form the basis for future attitudes and conduct. Contentment with being alone, inde-pendent decision-making, and self-sufficiency can be vital survival traits during the adolescent years.

If you find yourself continually rushing your child, as well as yourself, from one activity, errand or event to another, you are not alone. Consider how many conferences, regardless of their primary focus, include workshops on stress and time management. We are part of a rat-race culture, and our children are bearing the brunt of much of the pressure we put on ourselves and pass along to them. It is counterproductive to allow children to experience pressures at an early age in an attempt to "prepare them for the future." They will face the demands of life in the 21st century soon enough.

A major shift in the pace of American families is the result of a societal movement over the past several decades. Forty years ago, the vast majority of families had a full-time, stay-at-home parent. By contrast, at the beginning of the 21st century both parents were employed in 63 percent of two-parent families with children under 18.[5]

For some, the decision is based on the parent's making a deliberate choice between a career path and staying at home. For others, dual incomes are a perceived necessity, as managing on one income has become increasingly difficult due to the rising cost of living. If you fall into either category—choosing to work or feeling you have no choice—consider whether you could put a career on hold and manage with less income during your child's early years. Carefully calculating the expenses related to employment (e.g., child care, transportation costs, dining out, clothes) can be an enlightening exercise. Some parents discover that their job-related spending is actually greater than their take-home pay.

For more and more households, one paycheck is simply insufficient to provide the family's basic needs, and, unfortunately, those parents truly have no viable option other than dual employment. Likewise, for a growing number of single parents, full-time employment is a necessity, not a choice. The next couple of paragraphs are directed to parents who can manage to live on one household income while their children are young.

Let's step back for a moment and assess "sufficient" family income in the context of today's culture. Whether it pertains to cars, homes, vacations, the latest electronic toys, or all of the above, "bigger and better" has permeated American society. The accumulation of stuff is consciously and subconsciously affecting our thinking and driving our decisions. Many parental pairs believe they must both be employed in order to give their children "the best." Rather than defining what's best in terms of the accumulation of possessions, we must view it in terms of the quality of our present family life and the groundwork we are laying for future relationships with our children.

When my husband and I were young parents, an elderly preacher's visit to our church was most timely. We have never forgotten his wise and insightful statement on that Sunday morning more than four decades ago. His seven words were these: "Richness consists of your fewness of wants." At that juncture of our life, my husband's income was sufficient to meet the "needs" of a family of three, but it was nowhere close to sufficient to fulfill our "wants." We learned a lot about ourselves, possessions, and priorities during the first few years of our marriage.

Take a moment to contemplate the following questions regarding the pace and priorities in your home.

- How would I define the overall tempo of our family life? Are we strolling at a pace that allows us to enjoy what is going on around us or are we charging through life?
- How often do I use the word "hurry"? How often am I stressed as a result of time pressure?
- Does the pace of my life fit the physical and emotional needs of me and my children? Do I notice what is going on around me?
- If I am rushing, what are the causes? Too many parental commitments? Too many children's activities? Both?
- When I enroll my child in an activity, is it for myself or for my child? (Do I take pride in telling others that my

three-year-old is in gymnastics? Do I believe that somehow reflects positively on my parenting?)
- Before I make a work-related or volunteer commitment, do I carefully consider its impact on myself and my children?
- Do my spouse and/or I need to cut back on the time and energy we devote to employment? Have we honestly assessed our family's needs vs. our wants?
- Are there any pragmatic, deliberate changes I need to make so that my home and family life is more comfortably paced?
- If changes are needed, am I willing to make them?

Before I leave this topic, I want to remind you that the hours, the days, the weeks, the months, and even the years, are very quickly here and gone. There's never a second chance to experience them. Listen to and trust the voice of a mother whose children are grown. Someday you will look back and wonder where those priceless childhood years have gone.

You will ask yourself whether you took the time to fully appreciate and enjoy each stage of life as much as you could have—and should have. I often think of the lyrics of the song titled "Turn Around": "Where are you going, my little one, little one? Where are you going, my baby, my own? Turn around and you're two, turn around and you're four, turn around and you're a young girl going out of my door. . . . Turn around and you're tiny, turn around and you're grown, turn around and you're a young wife with babes of your own."[6]

For the sake of your children, as well as yourself, don't wait until tomorrow to slow down and truly cherish the fast-fleeting moments of childhood.

ROUTINES AND RITUALS

In giving instructions to church leadership, the Apostle Paul wrote that "everything should be done in [an] . . . orderly way."[7]

This advice is well taken not just for churches, but for homes as well—especially those that include young children. Predictability breeds security and promotes well-being. Children's biological and emotional internal clocks function best with regular routines.

Regularity involves not only *when* a particular routine will take place, but also *who* will participate and *what* will occur. Family mealtimes, which provide natural opportunities for cohesion, don't just happen. Particularly as children get older, merely getting all members to the table simultaneously can be difficult.

Beyond physical togetherness, mealtimes can serve as an energizing and restoring touch point—a time for children and parents to share their day's delights and concerns in a safe, caring atmosphere, free of criticism, arguing, and reprimanding. Mealtimes should be happy, conducive to enjoyment of the company as well as the food. (Have you ever wondered why in some homes singing at the table is not permitted? Doesn't it seem that it might be more appropriate for singing to be *required*?)

Research points out a further benefit of family meals: The family eating meals together has been shown to be a protective factor against adolescent girls' disordered eating, such as extreme weight control measures and binge eating.[8]

As another example, regardless of what has transpired during the day, a one-on-one, peaceful bedtime routine—a short story, a song and a prayer—can serve as a balm and promote bonding between parent and child. Daily routines offer unlimited opportunities for family members to share significant moments of time.

Through rituals and routines, parents have the privilege of defining and designing the meaning of being a member of a particular family. As young children become preadolescents and begin moving in circles beyond the family, memories of traditions and celebrations sustain feelings of belonging. In addition to regular routines, activities such as summer vacations on the beach, 4th of

July fireworks, Thanksgiving food baskets for a family in need, Christmas Eve candlelight services, and New Year's Day brunches all serve to promote warmth, familiarity, and connectedness among family members.

Birthday celebrations are a great opportunity to honor individual family members. The "birthday boy" or "birthday girl" (even if an adult) should feel especially loved and appreciated. Along with fun surprises that include the honoree's favorites, traditions that everyone shares enhance a family's feelings of unity and oneness.

Our family has carried on a birthday tradition that began several generations ago. Celebrations include singing three verses of "Happy Birthday" and eating white nut cake with Aunt Dorothy's icing. Several years ago someone, relatively new to our family by marriage, was attending his first family party. After hearing us discuss the cake and icing with great enthusiasm, he asked, "Have I met Aunt Dorothy?" No, he hadn't. And at that point we all realized that *none* of us, other than our mother, had any recollection of her. What we did know is that she made delicious icing and, more importantly, provided our family with a unique birthday tradition.

Perhaps you are wondering why I have spent several paragraphs stating the obvious. Doesn't everyone know that the family should eat meals together and children should feel special on their birthdays?

First, there is a vast difference between knowing something intellectually and being sufficiently convinced of its importance to put it into practice. We need to be reminded that routines, shared activities, rituals, intentional family patterns and traditions—by *any* name—require thoughtfulness, planning, and priority status.

Second, chances are I would not view this topic as so significant had it not emerged as a glaring missing ingredient in the homes of the troubled teens I interviewed. One said, "We really never did a family activity or anything like that." Another told me birthdays "really stand out" because those were the only times during the entire year the family ate dinner and played games together. Still another concluded that her family did have a "routine," as they yelled at each other at least once a night.

As strongly as I have just defended the cause of family rituals, I would be remiss if I didn't add a caveat. I caution you to not force an activity on your family simply for the sake of routine, because a friend told you how much her family likes it, or because you remember enjoying it when you were a child. If something's not working, let it go.

In addition, don't adhere to rituals or traditions so dogmatically that you lose your sense of perspective. If you, Mom and Dad, have the opportunity to take a Caribbean cruise, don't decline because someone else (or maybe even no one) would be reading your children a bedtime story for seven days. Routines without flexibility are hard to distinguish from hard-nosed, legalistic demands, which eventually put wedges in relationships, rather than solidifying them.

HAVING FUN

When one of our sons was in third grade, his teacher gave his class the following assignment: "What is your favorite place? Write about it." Our son's response was brief and to the point: "I like to be at home. It's fun there and it's always welcoming." When I recently pulled the weathered notebook page from my memorabilia file, I took a moment to reflect on those penciled words of some 27 years ago. The teacher's smiley face at the top of the page was no match for my own. I'm sure he didn't always view being at home as quite so desirable, but at least on that particular day my son answered the question the way I would have hoped.

What makes home a child's favorite place? At least in part, I believe it's the ambience—how a home "feels." Balloons for no particular reason, the smell of cookies fresh out of the oven, a book of Calvin and Hobbes on the coffee table, singing while doing dishes, sitting on the porch swing, welcome-home hugs, lively mealtime conversations, and, most certainly, laughter. A joyful home atmosphere promotes inner health and provides a haven and healing for the wounded, for, after all: "A cheerful heart is good medicine."[9]

Part of the art of family fun is learning to enjoy the little, spontaneous moments of life, and laughing together—and at oneself. "Inside" humorous stories occur naturally over time and bind family members' lives on a level none other share, thus reinforcing a sense of unity and belonging. I suggest keeping a journal, or just a spiral notebook, convenient at all times, for the express purpose of recording family humor.

Sadly, many of the teens with whom I spoke had no memories of their homes being happy *or* fun. Rather, they wanted to spend as little time at home as possible. How very sad when children leave home because they dislike the people who live there.

Even children who enjoy their families begin to spend less time at home and more time with their peers during adolescence. This is as it should be; it's part of growing up and is consistent with the new level of social and emotional autonomy for which they are striving. As one adult—no doubt the parent of a teen—comically observes: "The best way to keep kids at home is to make the home a pleasant atmosphere . . . and to let the air out of their tires." Moving away from the familiar nest called home is normal, expected, and desired. But when angry children storm or sneak out the back door as a means of escape, it is evident they don't perceive their home as a refuge.

TIME FOR SPOUSE AND SELF

Let's recap. Our homes should be fun-filled, orderly and stress-free havens in which our children can smile and grow. We, as parents, must selflessly throw our entire beings into making that ideal a reality. What a perfect plan, assuming that we as adults are super-human and have no needs of our own. Trying to be all things to all people all the time simply does not work out for mere mortals. I know, because I've tried.

The home environment is less than optimal when the needs of any family member, child or adult, are ignored. In two-parent homes, part of creating a positive home environment for our children is conscientiously cultivating the relationship between the parents. Let me speak specifically to mothers here since that's the role to which I can relate. Putting our children's wants before those of our husband's is something to which many of us are prone. His needs may not be as obvious or seem as urgent as rocking a fussy baby or teaching a toddler to share her animal crackers.

Nevertheless, we must remain aware of, and sensitive to, how easy it is for our children's needs to take precedent over those of our husband. I truly believe this phenomenon is at least partially to blame for the high rate of divorce. Jointly raising children tends to draw you together or drive you apart. I encourage you to strive for the former with passion and intentionality.

Looking beyond the present, when the pitter-patter of little feet running down the hall is nothing but a distant memory, you and the person with whom you share the morning paper, the toothpaste tube, and the leftover casseroles should still be intimately and emotionally embracing life together. Every day we make decisions (be they conscious, or subconscious) of whether we will foster or neglect this relationship that formed the very foundation of our family.

Finally, you may have heard this definition of JOY: "Jesus first, Others second, and Yourself last." Generally, that's a good principle for Christian parenting, since God should be first in our lives and selflessness seems to be an essential quality to adequately fulfilling a parental role. However, if we as parents allow our emotional, physical, and spiritual resources to become totally depleted, we cannot even begin to create a healthy environment for the other members of our family. Sometimes we don't even realize that we're neglecting ourselves.

We simply must take time for renewal of our own bodies, souls, and spirits in order to meet the needs of those we love. Throwing pebbles into a brook, soaking in a bubble bath, listening to our favorite music, having tea with a close friend, sensing God's presence through quiet time with Him—there are endless ways to be sure we aren't continually giving of ourselves without replenishing our inward resources.

How comfortable would we be sailing on a ship whose captain consistently worked 18-hour days, leaving little time for physical renewal and no time at all for social and emotional support? Trying to give too much is unhealthy for us as well as for those who need us.

Chapter 9
TURBULENT SEAS

It is better to meet danger than to wait for it. He that is on a lee shore, and foresees a hurricane,
stands out to sea and encounters a storm to avoid a shipwreck.
(CHARLES CALEB COLTON)[1]

As captains of our family's vessel, we generally feel that we have some control over what happens onboard—that is, within the four walls of our homes. But all too soon we must begin to prepare our children for the turbulent seas in the form of external forces that our ship and its occupants will inevitably encounter. When our children are young, selecting and controlling the influences in their lives is relatively manageable. But negative societal forces, over which we have little or no control, begin to have an impact on our children's thoughts, attitudes, and behaviors at a very early age.

No 21st-century parent needs to be told that countless forces threaten to disrupt America's families. Societal standards have deteriorated markedly over the past several decades and, when we no longer monitor our children 24/7, we can safely assume that they will encounter a value system very unlike the one we have attempted to instill. Who and what are these ominous adversaries of the family?

107

MEDIA

First we will look at a most powerful and invading force: technology. But before I continue, let me include one caveat. I'm hesitant to even begin to discuss such a rapidly changing landscape, as there will undoubtedly be a myriad of novel electronic gadgets on the market before the print on this publication has dried. Having said that, I would be doing a disfavor to you, the reader, to ignore such a potentially destructive phenomenon.

Simply put, media's broad influence is capable of leaving an indelible and devastating mark. Statistics indicate that all children, including the very young, are spending more time than ever in front of a screen.[2]

Mobile devices, with limitless apps and addictive powers that keep young minds engaged for hours, now supplement television viewing as electronic babysitters. The continual parental modeling of mobile device use while shopping, driving, walking, doing household chores, and eating dinner further reinforces its influence on the young.

Considering just the quantity of children's engagement with electronic media, there is cause for concern. But what about quality? Their senses as well as their minds are processing a myriad of messages from sources with far different objectives than the ones we have in mind for our children.

Let's begin with a discussion of potential negative repercussions of media use that have nothing to do with content. For instance, children's habitual engagement with electronic media can lead to their becoming observers *of* life rather than participants *in* life. They expect the world to amuse, engage, and entertain them at a fast-moving and exhilarating pace. Beyond increasing children's expectations of learning delivered via entertainment, media use lessens the time children read, thus increasing the probability their academic performance will be compromised.

Media entertainment can also become a substitute for family socialization. Chosen carefully and used sparingly, movies and television can be an acceptable family pastime. However, when family members are seated side-by-side with a screen—rather than each other—as the focus, meaningful interaction, communication, and problem-solving are conspicuously absent.

Further concern about media use pertains to childhood obesity, which is rising at an alarming rate and has frightening ramifications for our children's future well-being. Multiple studies have linked childhood obesity and media, simply because more and more children are engaging in sedentary, rather than active, lifestyles. The incidence of Type II diabetes, which is associated with obesity, has quadrupled in the last two decades.

As we move on to the *content* of electronic experiences to which our children are exposed, perhaps you're thinking you have heard all there is to say on this topic—and maybe you have. But please indulge me a few paragraphs to impress upon you the importance of parental vigilance and control.

Violence pervades the media world. How traumatizing to young children—who are developmentally unable to distinguish between fantasy and reality—to see delightfully intriguing animated characters being choked, shot, stabbed and blown apart. Seeing few or no negative consequences, children begin to perceive violence as an acceptable and possibly desirable way to settle real-life conflict.

Viewing countless acts of violence has been consistently shown to cause children to become desensitized—and therefore less sympathetic—to victims of real-life violence. Furthermore, it increases their fears that they themselves will become victims.

Electronic media in which children are actively engaged—in contrast to television and movies where they are simply spectators—has often been defended because of its interactive and educational nature. But there's reason to believe that the impact of these devices is potentially more negative than viewing violence. With interactive media games, our children are not just being entertained by *watching* graphically played-out violence; through simulation, it's as if they are actually perpetrating the crimes.

In World War II, when soldiers in training shot at nonhuman targets, only 20 percent of them could bring themselves to shoot rifles at the enemy when they first went into combat. By contrast, 90 percent of today's first-time soldiers are able to shoot at the enemy. One of the most plausible explanations is that, through simulation, soldiers are now practicing to shoot at humans. When a child plays an interactive video game, he is learning to perfect the same conditioned reflex skills as a soldier in training.[3, 4]

Sadly, we know all too well it is not only soldiers who perfect the art of shooting to kill. School shootings, appalling and senseless acts of violence, have become an all-too-familiar phenomenon in America. As we look for common threads among these horrific crimes, the perpetrator's fascination with video games and the Internet is a theme that clearly emerges.

Please hear me clearly. I am not suggesting that every child who engages in violent video games will become comfortable with the thought of taking another's life. But we must be aware of the potential danger when children's natural inhibitions are broken down.

The internet is a form of media whose extensive impact we are just beginning to comprehend. Like other technology, it is an attractive, interactive, invigorating, and potentially addictive medium. Younger and younger children are becoming adept at using the internet for emailing, voice and video chatting, playing games, listening to music, doing homework, and selecting items for purchase from literally thousands of options.

Perfectly suited to a hurry-up world that thrives on instant gratification and welcomes the rush of superficial encounters, the internet provides immediate answers, on-the-spot entertainment, and overnight delivery. But for all its convenience and potential for making our lives more efficient and enjoyable, we all readily recognize that the internet can lead children down a very sinister path.

In seconds, impressionable and vulnerable children have access to subject matter such as instructions for building bombs; chat rooms that glorify and magnify the worst in the socially alienated, angry, downtrodden, and dysfunctional; and adult-only sites replete with pornographic scenes and subject matter.

The 1999 Columbine school massacre in which 13 people were killed and 26 wounded should have been a wake-up call for all of us. A tragic historical example of the internet's dark side, teenagers Eric Harris and Dylan Klebold eventually amassed an arsenal that included an assortment of guns and knives, along with 99 explosive devices, many of which were built from readily available internet recipes. As noted previously, this was one in a string of unthinkable mass murders that have gripped our country in recent decades.

As is no doubt evident, I simply cannot overstate what I believe to be the importance of adult monitoring of children's access to, and activity on, the internet.

On the topic of children's movies, I will begin with the bottom line, literally as well as figuratively. I believe that the production of movies targeted toward children is primarily about expanding financial conglomerates and not about providing wholesome family entertainment.

No one can deny the skill with which producers of children's movies have amassed millions of loyal followers, escorting viewers of all ages into an enchanting world of make-believe and magic. But it seems that we as a society have become so enthralled by the aura of fictional characters that we blindly endorse children's movies, based on their entertainment value, without carefully scrutinizing their content.

Personally, I would be much more comfortable with many of today's movies if they weren't marketed to young children. But I can scarcely endure to sit in a theater of young children while they watch their animated heroes encounter multiple traumatic and life-threatening events (accompanied by appropriately dramatic background crescendos). Children's cognitive development is nowhere near sophisticated enough to satisfactorily process and assimilate what their senses are taking in.

Why do parents choose to take their children to movies that are so emotionally intense? I reason that they must believe the movie is child-appropriate because it was promoted as such. Again, we must remind ourselves that the marketers of children's movies do not necessarily have their tiny consumers' well-being as top priority.

May I suggest that the next time you're tempted to "treat" your children to the latest movie that you consider another option, which admittedly requires more forethought and energy than driving to a theater and purchasing tickets and popcorn. Consider instead giving your child the choice of options such as having a picnic at a nearby park, visiting the children's area of the local library, playing Candy Land, building a birdhouse, or baking chocolate cupcakes.

MATERIALISM

Another pervading cultural influence is promotion of materialism. Why do supposedly family-friendly corporations market children's products that are potentially harmful? Why are children continually bombarded with advertising that creates an insatiable appetite for things? Let me quote a phrase I've heard my husband use many times in an effort to explain various phenomena: "Just follow the money trail." If you want to attempt to understand what drives individuals, families, and societies, determine the financial implications of their actions. In light of that, consider the relevance of this biblical warning written more than 1,900 years ago: "The love of money is a root of all kinds of evil."[5]

Society's love affair with affluence and its accompanying power has affected all American families. Those with young children have been hit especially hard by advertising that typifies a greed-over-principle mind-set.

Here's a case in point. A creator of an extremely violent first-person shooting game with a rating of "mature" openly admits that his goal is to sell it to young children. He's quoted as saying, "It'd be suicide to make the game unplayable by younger people." It occurs to me that "suicide" is an interesting choice of words.[6]

If it seems that marketers know exactly how to entrap your children in the mire of desire and its accompanying whining, you're not experiencing paranoia. Major market research firms hire consultants whose sole purpose is to rate children's products according to their "nag factor"—the capacity to cause children to beg. For corporations like McDonald's, Toys R Us, and Disney, winning the battle for our children's loyalty, and consequently our dollars, is paramount to their bottom line.[7, 8]

In my opinion, one of the most frightening aspects of this marketing phenomenon is the cult-like zeal of those who have perfected the art. According to those who truly understand the power of marketing to children, when six-month-old babies are beginning to say "mama" and "dada," they are forming mental images of corporate logos and mascots.[9] The exploitation of even society's tiniest citizens translates into big bucks for big business.

As in every other aspect of parenting, doing what is right for our children in the long term, as opposed to taking the path of least resistance at the moment, is never easy. As noted earlier, evidence leads us to believe that parents are getting less and less adept at saying "no." "Keeping up with the Joneses" appears to be alive and well; and "I deserve because I exist" has become the mantra of many young children.

A well-known psychologist has this to say about child indulgence: "If you never allow a child to want something, he never enjoys the pleasure of receiving it."[10]

The exploitation of children's innocence and vulnerabilities by the cleverest marketing minds is just one societal force that has made parenting more difficult with each subsequent generation. There is so much more for children to want, and denying them is harder than ever before. Additionally, because they are likely to spend more hours at work, parents are eager to do whatever it takes to maintain a relatively conflict-free home atmosphere. And, at least sometimes, calming a storm requires a "yes," even when parents know they should say "no."

Another issue related to the problem of materialism is the question of how these children, who are accustomed to getting whatever they desire, will be able to monitor their own spending as they get older. Is there any reason to believe they will somehow become persons characterized by self-control and contentment?

In spite of all of these concerns, I am hopeful the pendulum is about to begin swinging in the opposite direction. As the phenomenon of materialism and excess reaches all-time highs, it appears that some parents are becoming more aware that they are doing their children no favors by indulging their every whim.

MUSIC

Music, in its various forms, has been a meaningful and powerful influence since the beginning of time. In today's world, perhaps as much as in any other era, music has become a means of expressing ideologies and motivating actions. Music draws converts, if you will, to a particular way of viewing life. Equally important to its ideology is music's ability to provide a sense of identity and an accepting clique of fellow followers, a much sought-after commodity among America's children and youth.

There are multiple examples of particular music icons and genres becoming a culture within a culture as they permeate and dictate their groupies' thoughts, moods, speech, behaviors, mannerisms, and belief system. The power of the medium of music should not be underestimated. Many of the teens I interviewed support this premise.

One teen told me that he and his friends were drug dealers because of greed. "It's just like they say in rap," he said. "Greed, money, sex. . . . They wouldn't rap about it if they didn't love it." Other teens spoke of their attitudes getting worse, even to the point of getting involved in fist fights, when they listened to pop icons whose lyrics center on hatred, rage, and violence.

Several of the teens expressed the opinion that music does not precipitate negative behavior, but does reinforce it. They admitted that some music gave them evil feelings. Those "evil feelings" appear to be similar to the "aggression-related thoughts and emotions" that were the focus of a study involving 500 college students and their choice of music. Without regard to differences in musical style or the specific performing artist, violent songs—even humorous ones—increased feelings of hostility without provocation or threat. Needless to say, as aggressive thoughts escalate, so do accompanying aggressive behaviors.[11]

Music is a great example of a medium that can have either negative or positive effects. There is so much good music to which our children can be exposed, even at very young ages, and it is our responsibility to make this happen.

ROLE MODELS

Societial standards are clearly reflected in all forms of technology, including television shows, movies, and music. The ever-declining norms are personified in not only the roles, but also the real lives, of many of the pop stars our children idolize and imitate. Indulgence, self-centeredness, addictive behaviors, promiscuity, and lack of commitment are not only tolerated, but encouraged. Familiarity breeds contentment, so negative behavior becomes more and more acceptable to our children simply through exposure. Further, due to the phenomenon of age compression, children are "getting older younger," and are thus embracing cultural norms at an earlier age than ever before.

PEERS

The power of peer pressure is directly related to the societal forces just discussed. In our analogy of a voyage, peers entering the picture can be likened to buccaneers on board. Although peer influence is certainly not all negative, the reality is that family dynamics invariably change as additional relationships are added to the parent-child mix.

If your children are very young, you aren't yet dealing with the ramifications of their having friends other than those you have chosen. But now is the time to begin thinking about what to expect so you can be proactive, rather than reactive, in dealing with this potentially powerful force in your children's lives. As early as preschool, many children begin to get their cues on how to talk, act, and look from their peers. Although the transition is rather gradual, this apparent shift of allegiance from parent to peer seems to catch many parents off guard.

Very rare is the 12- or 13-year-old who does not gravitate toward peers, seeing their approval and acceptance as infinitely more important than that of their parents. Of course, peer pressure is not inherently bad. Just as our children's friends can influence them negatively, they can also do so positively. Friends who share our values, beliefs, and standards provide a very powerful protective factor for our children.

We all know that regardless of what we say or do, there are no guarantees that our children will not hang out with the "wrong crowd," anymore than we can promise our best friend that our toddler will never again bite her toddler. But we *can* be sure that following certain parenting principles will reduce the likelihood that our children will make poor choices when it comes to the selection of friends.

As discussed earlier, an overarching protective factor is one of family connectedness, characterized by mutual unconditional loving, caring, and respect. Additionally, loving but firm discipline and monitoring help our children make wise choices regarding the friends they choose. We can also affect our children's peer selection in a more direct manner.

When our children are young, we have a great deal of control over when, where, how, and with whom they spend their time. By choosing to expose them to particular people and environments, we provide our children with early experiences that form the basis of their future decisions regarding relationships.

For example, when we take our children to church and enroll them in church-related activities, they become friends with others whose families are likely to share our beliefs and values. Our impressionable young children are dependent on us to give direction and make wise choices regarding their peer selection. This, of course, changes over time. Consider the contrast of parental input regarding birthday invitees when our children are four, eight, and twelve years of age.

One of the most important ways we can influence our children's friendships is by the behavior we model. Hosting a toddler play group and backyard picnics with other families lets our children know that friends are important and our home is a place where they are welcomed. Although this may not be workable for every family, we had a standing policy in our home: Our children's friends were always welcome. We took the welcome mat on the front porch literally and wanted our children's friends to do so as well.

As our children get older and our influence lessens in terms of their choice of friends, what principles do we want them to have learned from us? Beyond setting the pattern (and expectation) that their friends spend time in our home, we need to be continually vigilant for opportunities to help them recognize positive traits in others.

This means that we are not only attempting to instill virtues such as kindness, goodness, and self-control in our own children, we are also teaching them to assess and appreciate these qualities in others.

Even if we wanted to—and although we are at times tempted to try—there is no way we can insulate our children from all external influences. Peer groups naturally form regardless of the type of schools or other activities our children attend. Outside the classroom, the vast majority of extracurricular activities and youth organizations are also structured around children's ages and interests.

Gradually, children begin to spend more and more time away from adult supervision and in the company of peers. By the time they are high school age, most teens are with their peers more than twice as much as they are with parents or other adults. Rather than trying to protect our children from any and all external influences, which is impossible, we must instead prepare them to make wise choices.

As we end our discussion on societal influences, let's return for a moment to the big picture—the people we hope our children will someday become.

Do we really believe that the plethora of technology and media offerings in today's world has the potential of negatively affecting our children's physical, cognitive, social, emotional, and spiritual development?

Are we willing to "unplug" our children from the bombardment of messages from those whose values differ greatly from our own?

Are we concerned that our children might "buy into" the notion that the values and behaviors of pop stars are the essence of happiness?

Do we stand ready to encourage our children's association with positive peers and discourage relationships that appear to be detrimental?

Assuming the answer to each of these questions is yes, we have ample motivation to rise to the level of authority figures with the fortitude to do what is best, not what is easiest, on behalf of our children.

Chapter 10
THE LIGHTHOUSE

He that will learn to pray, let him go to sea.
(GEORGE HERBERT)[1]

everal years ago, I heard a bluegrass band sing an old gospel song. One refrain from the song particularly struck me: "If it weren't for the Lighthouse, where would this ship be?"[2] Because I've already said it's a gospel song, you probably don't need to be told that the Lighthouse refers to God.

Often since I began writing this book I've thought back to the Irish fisherman's prayer, quoted in the beginning of chapter 1, and envisioned a tiny boat surrounded by a huge expanse of water, looking a bit adrift and maybe even forlorn (assuming a boat could look that way). How heartening to add to that visual an utterly dependable Lighthouse off on the horizon, whose sole purpose is to guide that small and seemingly insignificant boat safely to its destination.

God not only guides us on a daily basis, He also provides lifelines for us when we're none too sure our boat is going to stay afloat. The lifelines that I will address here are ones that I have found particularly meaningful in my own parenting journey: faith, prayer, the Bible, and others. I will begin with faith as it seems to be foundational. Without faith there's really no point in reading the Bible or praying.

Although this chapter is written with an emphasis on the importance of a spiritual Presence in our lives, I encourage those of you who don't necessarily agree with that premise to read on. Perhaps you will glean something meaningful and worthwhile.

FAITH

Faith allows us to rely on Someone other than ourselves or any other mere mortal. Take, for instance, the biblical story of the Israelites who found themselves in exile, wandering aimlessly. How reassuring it must have been for them to hear their Father God declaring, "I know the plans I have for you . . . plans to prosper you and not to harm you, plans to give you hope and a future."[3] Through faith, we can claim this promise not only for ourselves but for our children as well.

Even when our daily lives and our concept of an ideal family seem to bear no resemblance to each other, the same God who reassured the Israelites also has plans "to prosper and not to harm" our families. If this is true, perhaps you wonder why bad things happen to good people. So do I. Rather than delve into a theological discussion for which I'm totally unqualified regarding the sovereignty and purposes of God, I'll simply say that when circumstances don't make sense, faith enters.

Faith allows us to cling to the promise that God always has our good in mind, regardless of how things look from our very limited, human perspective. This explanation is consistent with the Bible's definition of faith: "confidence in what we hope for and assurance about what we do not see."[4]

Faith in God also means acknowledging that He knows—even better than we do—what's best for our children. Even though many of us would accept this from an intellectual or theoretical perspective, practically we might find it very hard to believe. When one of our sons was going through a particularly rough time, I just wanted God to rescue him. After all, God *is* God, which means He can do anything.

My prayers were full of suggestions regarding how God could fix the problem. Then, through the words of a worship song, God spoke to me in a very forceful way.

It's all about You, Jesus, and all this is for You

For Your glory and Your fame.

It's not about me, as if You should do things my way

You alone are God and I surrender to Your ways.[5]

"You alone are God and I surrender to Your ways." Easier said than done! I had to repeat this phrase over and over and over until I was, at least in some small way, ready to "let go and let God." When it comes to our children, surrendering our own hopes and dreams is incredibly difficult.

THE BIBLE

Reliance on the Bible and faith are inseparable, for it's only by faith we can claim the literally thousands of promises it contains. Replete with words and imageries to encourage, support, and assist us, the Bible is a resource that most of us tap into much too infrequently. Its relevance and applicability seem to become particularly apparent when we feel the most anxious or inadequate. In addition to the verses mentioned previously in this book, let me share just a few that served as lifelines in my parenting journey and continue to do so to this day.

When emotional and physical exhaustion take their toll:

- "But those who hope in the LORD will renew their strength. They will soar on wings like eagles; they will run and not grow weary, they will walk and not be faint."[6]

When nothing's making sense and disappointment and disillusionment begin to set in:

- "'For my thoughts are not your thoughts, neither are your ways my ways,' declares the LORD. 'As the heavens are higher than the earth, so are my ways higher than your ways and my thoughts than your thoughts.'"[7]

When my soul is anything but peaceful:
- "You will keep in perfect peace those whose minds are steadfast, because they trust in you."[8]

When I'm worried about what might happen today:
- "Don't fret or worry. Instead of worrying, pray. Let petitions and praises shape your worries into prayers, letting God know your concerns."[9]

When I'm worried about what might happen tomorrow:
- "Give your entire attention to what God is doing right now, and don't get worked up about what may or may not happen tomorrow. God will help you deal with whatever hard things come up when the time comes."[10]

When my faith is waning:
- "Nothing, you see, is impossible with God."[11]

When my confidence is shaken:
- "I will praise the LORD, who counsels me; even at night my heart instructs me. I keep my eyes always on the LORD. With him at my right hand, I will not be shaken."[12]

When I wonder if God really cares about me and my family:
- "Are not five sparrows sold for two pennies? Yet not one of them is forgotten by God. Indeed, the very hairs of your head are all numbered. Don't be afraid; you are worth more than many sparrows."[13]

When I feel the need to fix things myself:
- "In quietness and trust is your strength."[14]

When I question whether peacemaking is worth the effort:
- "If it is possible, as far as it depends on you, live at peace with everyone."[15]

When I need a reminder of what others, and particularly my children, should be seeing in me:
- "So, chosen by God for this new life of love, dress in the wardrobe God picked out for you: compassion, kindness, humility, quiet strength, discipline."[16]

PRAYER

Although we previously talked about praying for and with our children, I am defining "lifeline prayers" as those that we utter when it seems like we and/or our children are about to go under for the third time.

As I look back over the years that my husband and I have been parents, there were several instances when I had a sense of despair—wracked with fear that something terrible was going to happen to our child. One of our sons was hospitalized as an infant, and we helplessly stood by watching the nurse tie him down with strips of green fabric and prick his tiny arm to begin intravenous feeding. He looked at us pleadingly and screamed for us to rescue him, but we could do nothing. Nothing but leave him and his future in the loving care of the One who had given him to us in the first place.

The example of our son's illness is likely one to which most parents relate, at least to some degree. But none of us are naïve enough to think that our children's health will be our only, or even necessarily our greatest, concern. Any seasoned parent will tell you that there are countless "opportunities" for distress, such as a first grader who can't read, a 10-year-old who seems to have no friends, or a 13-year-old who will do whatever it takes to be accepted by peers. Regardless of the situation, lifeline prayers shift the burden from our shoulders to those of an omnipotent being. Whew!

The book of Psalms records hundreds of David's lifeline prayers that serve as a model for us. Frequently David simply poured out his heart to God, both when he sensed his helplessness to face his circumstances and when he became overcome by God's goodness to him. I will share a few of David's prayers that are particularly meaningful to me. I encourage you to dig through Psalms (and elsewhere in the Bible) to find lifeline prayers that suit your own deepest needs.

- "How long must I wrestle with my thoughts and day after day have sorrow in my heart? . . . Look on me and answer, LORD my God."[17]
- "Have mercy on me, my God, have mercy on me, for in you I take refuge. I will take refuge in the shadow of your wings."[18]
- "When I am afraid, I put my trust in you."[19]
- "Show me your ways, LORD, teach me your paths. Guide me in your truth and teach me, for you are God my Savior, and my hope is in you all day long."[20]
- "When I said, 'My foot is slipping,' your unfailing love, LORD, supported me. When anxiety was great within me, your consolation brought me joy."[21]
- "I sought the LORD, and he answered me; he delivered me from all my fears."[22]
- "I will exalt you, LORD, for you lifted me out of the depths."[23]
- "You, God, are awesome."[24]

OTHERS

Along with Bible reading and prayer, there's another powerful source of strength and encouragement on which we can draw.

Having those in our lives with whom we can share our greatest joys and deepest concerns is an invaluable lifeline when fog obscures our path or angry waves threaten to pull us under.

Seeking counsel and comfort requires that we admit (to ourselves and others) that everything is not perfect in our little world. With so much of our own self-worth tied up in our children, vulnerability is painful. But we were not made to live in isolation. True friends, who share our values and hopes and understand our struggles, won't provide hollow reassurances or trite answers. But they will lend a listening ear and a soft shoulder, along with much-needed objectivity, perspective, and hope.

As we head toward the gleam of the Lighthouse, a stubborn faith, relentless prayer, the promises of the Bible, and a network of supportive friends serve to reassure us that perhaps the boat isn't quite so small or the sea as wide as it appears to us at the moment.

Chapter 11
ENJOYING THE JOURNEY

*One hundred years from now it will not matter what kind of car
I drove, what kind of house I lived in, how much money
I had in my bank account, nor what my clothes looked like.
But one hundred years from now, the world may be a little better
because I was important in the life of a child.*

(AUTHOR UNKNOWN)

A s we come to the end of this brief book, my hope is that you feel encouraged and energized. Perhaps some of the principles presented in the previous pages reinforced your philosophy of parenting—yes, you do have a philosophy, even if you've never thought of it as such—and your resolve to give this complex and potentially trying task your very best shot. Perhaps you've decided to make some changes in the way you parent; if so, I trust you are motivated by optimism rather than guilt. Regardless, my prayer is that you close this book convinced of how important you are in the life of your children and, possibly, many other children as well.

Now let me end with a word of caution. As much as I've encouraged you to pour yourself into these parenting years, I want also to urge you to enjoy the journey along the way. Many vacationers choose the quickest mode of getting from point A to point B and look at their destination as the point in time at which the fun begins.

Old-fashioned road trips have given way to bustling airports, cranky travelers, and miniature packages of pretzels. Of course, efficiency is often a major consideration because the one thing we never seem to have enough of is leisurely time. But, in this hurry-up world, the joy of the journey itself seems to be too frequently sacrificed on the altar of expediency. So it can be with parenting.

Yes, parenting is a mammoth task. Yes, we are our children's providers, advocates, protectors, and primary source of self-esteem and identity. Yes, today's parenting decisions need to be governed by long-term plans and goals. Yes, it's a scary world out there. But to see parenting as an overwhelming 24/7 responsibility, with only a very occasional carefree moment, is to risk missing innumerable joys and countless memorable moments. My final thoughts and suggestions pertain to what I refer to as parenting with a balanced perspective.

Having set the course of your family's journey, relax and take a day—even a moment—at a time, rather than living under a veil of concerns for your children's future. Remember to pick some daisies and smell some roses. And keep your sense of humor. I'm not sure of its origin, but a little expression that has helped me attempt to keep life's relatively insignificant incidents in perspective is, "Some day we'll look back and laugh; so why not laugh now?"

Remember that the little hassles of parenting young children are just that: little hassles. When I was director of our church nursery, I was checking in infants and toddlers so their mothers could attend a weekly two-hour parenting study and discussion group. This hardly comes as a newsflash, but nine o'clock in the morning can seem quite early to young mothers. Some arrived a few minutes early, some on time, and most arrived after the scheduled beginning time.

One was quite late; she came at 9:45 with her two little girls, a five-month-old in a carrier and an 18-month-old toddler hanging on to her momma's coattail. The mother's body language and facial expressions indicated it had been a rough morning. The little ones were soon situated in their respective rooms and their mother was writing instructions for the caregivers. When she looked up, she had big tears in her eyes. With a sigh, she said simply, "It seems like I'll never, ever get anywhere on time."

My response was just as simple: "I know it seems that way right now. Let me give you a hug." This gesture of understanding and caring seemed to rejuvenate her, at least for the moment.

This young mother's frustration should in no way be trivialized. Maybe other mothers could arrive on time, but no matter how hard she tried, it seemed beyond her ability to do so. At that moment, her feelings of inadequacy were overwhelming.

Attempt to keep a balanced perspective. No parents or children, even "the best," are perfect. Don't put unrealistic expectations on yourself or on them. Years ago there was a commercial on television promoting a particular brand of children's shampoo. Here's a mother's testimonial: "The shampoo went into his eyes and he cried. I felt like a failure." If shampoo in her son's eyes caused her to feel like a failure, I predict this mother had quite a rough road ahead.

Take time for yourself, to renew and refresh your energy, enthusiasm, and outlook. Don't become so wrapped up in your parenting role that you lose your own sense of self. Research repeatedly indicates what we would assume: The empty nest syndrome is very difficult for parents who, for the past 20 years, have used the quality and/or quantity of their parenting to gauge their own self-worth. As a reminder, "Kids with parents who have a life learn both that they aren't the center of the universe and that they can be free to pursue their own dreams."[1] Maintaining your sense of self is not just good for you; it's good for your children as well.

Never forget that you are engaged in one of the most important responsibilities in the world: raising your children. Assuming you want to do so, you have plenty of years ahead to live in a spotless house, cook a gourmet meal, and enjoy a leisurely, child-free lunch with a friend. Although teaching a child to say "please" and putting Spiderman Band-Aids® on skinned knees draw little attention or acclaim, the long-term significance may be greater than a multi-million dollar corporate deal closed by a CEO comfortably seated in an overstuffed leather chair in some palatial office. Do you really believe this? I do.

If you are a parent of young children, remember that a sense of efficiency or accomplishment can be quite illusive. Some days there's very little tangible evidence—if any at all—of the energy and effort that was expended.

In terms of household chores, you might have done two batches of laundry, cleaned part of the house, and eventually fed everyone who was hungry. So what's the state of the household at bedtime? There's dirty laundry heaped on the washing machine, muddy footprints all the way from the back door to the guest bath, and dirty dishes piled high in the sink and spilling over onto the counter.

Remind yourself that even if your day's urgent list has few items checked off, the really important stuff got done. You wiped runny noses, picked a bouquet of weeds, read your child's favorite storybook five times, attempted to explain where God lives, and kissed away tears. Now go peek in on your bear-hugging toddler in her ladybug sleeper and realize that this picture of absolute innocence and contentment reflects a parent's job well done. Savor the moment.

An unknown author has captured the essence and awe of childhood. "Believe in children. There is faith in their eyes, love in their touch, kindness in their gestures. Thrill with them at life's big and small moments. Hold them close."

Rather than continually attempting to disseminate wisdom to our children, we should also be listening, observing and drinking in the freshness of their insights and outlooks. Some of the greatest lessons of life can be learned from, rather than taught to, children. Much can be gained by following children's example of simple trust, an unhurried pace, pleasure in little things, and forgiving spirits.

Know that the best parents in the world can't shield their children from every bump along the way. Nor should they try. When our children were young, a dear friend said something to me that has come to mind hundreds of times through the years: "We aren't growing hothouse tomatoes." This little phrase helped me tremendously as I attempted to come to grips with the fact that some of life's storms, from which I desperately wanted to shelter my children, were exactly what they needed in order to become stronger.

Perhaps the ultimate in perspective-taking is to attempt to grasp how quickly little children grow up. When young children demand nearly 24/7 attention and their needs seem to totally eclipse our own, we feel we will never have the luxury of coming up for air. But children do grow up.

In retrospect, most parents with grown children are struck by how quickly the years have flown by. Although some days—or even hours—may seem agonizingly long to you now, I encourage you to enjoy the journey. Before you realize what's happened, *you* will be the one looking back and wondering where the days, months, and years have gone.

EPILOGUE

God will help a seaman in a storm,
but the pilot must still remain at the wheel.
(GERMAN PROVERB)

I wrote the first chapter of this book as I was sitting on a sandy beach overlooking the beautiful Gulf of Mexico. And now, as I write these final words, once again I'm looking out over the majestic waters. As I sit in reverent awe, I contemplate a God who created the deep waters and the creatures within, a God who knows the number of the sands of the sea, a God whose voice the winds and the waves obey. In stark contrast, I think of my own relative insignificance and, yet, His personal care and concern for all of His creation, including you and me.

Yesterday the sea was calm and the sun shone brightly overhead. I enjoyed the serenity of walking on the beach, dipping my bare feet into the water's edge, and watching children's imaginations being transformed into majestic sand castles. Today, by contrast, the skies are dark, the wind is howling, and the huge waves appear angry as they relentlessly lap at the shore, shaping and reshaping the water's edge.

Yesterday a small boat could have sailed peacefully; today, the same boat would be mercilessly tossed about. So it is with your life—and mine. On some days the air is foggy, the waters choppy, and there's dissension among the crew. On others, the skies are clear and the waters calm. Regardless, having charted the course and prepared for the journey, we can approach unexplored waters with expectancy, confidence, and a resolve to keep our hands firmly on the helm.

NOTES

Chapter 1

[1] Galinsky, Ellen. *The Six Stages of Parenthood*. Boston: Addison-Wesley, 1987.

[2] *The Bible*. Isaiah 40:31.

[3] Ibid. James 1:5.

Chapter 2

[1] da Vinci. Italian Architect, Inventor, Writer, 1452–1519.

[2] *The Bible*. Luke 2:52.

[3] Francis of Assisi. Founder of Franciscan Order, 1181–1226.

[4] *The Bible*. Ephesians 5:1–2 (NKJV).

[5] Ibid. Deuteronomy 6:6.

[6] Ibid. Deuteronomy 6:7.

[7] Ibid. Joshua 24:14.

[8] Ibid. Joshua 24:15.

[9] Ibid.

[10] Harris, Judith. "Where Is the Child's Environment? A Group Socialization Theory of Development." *Psychological Review* 102 (3) (1995): 458–489.

Chapter 3

[1] Plato. *The Republic*. 360 BC.

[2] Bailey, Becky. *Conscious Discipline: 7 Basic Skills for Brain Smart Classroom Management*. Oviedo, FL: Loving Guidance, 2000.

3 Ibid.

4 Ibid.

5 "Self-Control," *Music Machine: Fruit of the Spirit CD*. Sparrow Records, 1977.

Chapter 4

1 Terence. Roman Comic Poet, 185–159 BC.

2 Brendgen, Mara, Vitaro, Frank, and William M. Bukowski. "Affiliation with delinquent friends: Contributions of parents, self-esteem, delinquent behavior, and rejection by peers." *Journal of Early Adolescence* 18:3 (1998): 244–265.

3 Resnick, Michael D., Bearman, Peter S., Blum, Robert Wm, Bauman, Karl E., Harris, Kathleen M., Jones, Jo, Tabor, Joyce, Beuhring, Trish, Sieving, Renee E., Shew, Marcia, Ireland, Marjorie, Bearinger, Linda H. and J. Richard Udry. "Protecting Adolescents from Harm." *Journal of the American Medical Association* 238 (1997): 223–232.

4 Ackard, Diann M., Neumark-Sztainer, Dianne, Story M, and C. Perry. "Parent-Child Connectedness and Behavioral and Emotional Health among Adolescents." *American Journal of Preventive Medicine*. 30:1 (2006 Jan): 59–66.

5 Samperi, K. *Celebrating Mothers: A Book of Appreciation*. Edited by Glorya Hale and Carol Kelly-Gangi, 17. New York: MetroBooks, 2002.

6 *The Bible*. 1 Corinthians 12:31 (NKJV).

7 *The Bible*. 1 Corinthians 13:4–7.

8 Garbarino, James and Claire Berdard. *Parents Under Siege*. New York: The Free Press, 2002.

9 Reeves, E. J. College President (Retired), 1933– .

10 Chapman, Gary. *The Five Love Languages*. Chicago: Moody Publishers/Northfield Publishing, 1996.

11 Garbarino and Berdard. *Parents Under Siege*.

Chapter 5

[1] Drucker, Peter. F. Author, 1909– .

[2] *The Bible.* James 1:19.

[3] Carlson, Richard. *Don't Sweat the Small Stuff with Your Family.* New York: Hyperion, 1998.

[4] Tillich, Paul. American Theologian, 1886–1965.

[5] *The Bible.* Luke 10:40–41.

[6] Ibid. James 1:19.

[7] Ibid.

[8] Ibid. James 3:9–10.

[9] Ibid. James 3:11.

[10] Ibid. 1 Corinthians 13:11.

[11] Gordon, Thomas. *Parent Effectiveness Training: The Proven Program for Raising Responsible Children.* New York: Crown Publishing Group, 2008.

[12] *The Bible.* Matthew 12:34 (NKJV).

Chapter 6

[1] von Goethe, Johann Wolfgang. German Playwright, 1749–1832.

[2] Edward VIII, Duke of Windsor, 1894–1972.

[3] Cloud, Henry and John Townsend. *Boundaries with Kids: When to Say Yes, How to Say No.* Grand Rapids, MI: Zondervan, 2008.

[4] *The Bible.* Ephesians 6:1.

[5] Merriam-Webster Online. www.m-w.com (accessed 7/19/13).

[6] Ibid.

[7] Kingsley, Charles. English Priest of Church of England, 1819–1875.

[8] Baumrind, Diana. "The influence of parenting style on adolescent competence and substance use." *Journal of Early Adolescence* 11 (1) (1991):56–95.

[9] Studies cited:

Lamborn, Susie D., Mounts, Nina S., Steinberg, Laurence and Dornbusch, S. M. "Patterns of Competence and Adjustment among Adolescents from Authoritative, Authoritarian, Indulgent, and Neglectful Families." *Child Development*, 62:1049–1065. doi: 10.1111/j.1467–8624.1991.tb01588.

Steinberg, Laurence, Blatt-Eisengart, Ilana, and Elizabeth Cauffman. "Patterns of Competence and Adjustment among Adolescents from Authoritative, Authoritarian, Indulgent, and Neglectful Homes: A Replication in a Sample of Serious Juvenile Offenders." *Journal of Research on Adolescence*.16: 47–58. doi: 10.1111/j.1532-7795.2006.00119.

Peiser, Nadine C., and Patrick C. L. Heaven. "Family Influences on Self-Reported Delinquency among High School Students." *Journal of Adolescence* 19 (1996):557–568.

Resnick, Michael D., Bearman, Peter S., Blum, Robert Wm, Bauman, Karl E., Harris, Kathleen M., Jones, Jo, Tabor, Joyce, Beuhring, Trish, Sieving, Renee E., Shew, Marcia, Ireland, Marjorie, Bearinger, Linda H. and J. Richard Udry. Protecting adolescents from harm. *Journal of the American Medical Association* 238 (1997): 223–232.

Weiss, Laura H., and J. Conrad Schwarz. "The Relationship between Parenting Types and Older Adolescents' Personality, Academic Achievement, Adjustment, and Substance Use. "*Child Development* 67 (1996): 2101–2114, http://onlinelibrary.wiley.com/doi/10.1111/j.14678624.1996.tb01846.

Boyes, M. C. and S. G. Allen. "Styles of Parent-Child Interaction and Moral Reasoning in Adolescence." *Merrill-Palmer Quarterly* 39:4 (1993): 551-570.

Klinzing, Dene Garvin. "Parenting Styles Can Influence Children." University of Delaware: UDAILY. http://www.udel.edu/PR/UDaily/2005/mar/style050305.html

[10] *The Bible*. 2 Chronicles 1:10.

11 Dobson, James. "Family Talk Parenting Devotional." http://www. oneplace.com/ministries/family-talk/read/devotionals/daily-devotions-for-parents-by-dr-james-dobson/dr-dobsons-parenting-devotional-june-8-11661454.html (accessed 7/19/13).

12 Dinkmeyer, Sr., Don C., Gary D. McKay, and Don C. Dinkmeyer, Jr. *The Parent's Handbook: Systematic Training for Effective Parenting.* Bowling Green, KY: STEP Publishers, 2007.

13 Bogenschneider, Karen, Wu, Ming-Yeh, Raffaelli, Marcela and Jenner C. Tsay. "Parent Influences on Adolescent Peer Orientation and Substance Use: The Interface of Parenting Practices and Values." *Child Development* 69:6 (1998): 1672–88.

Chapter 7

1 Calloway, Bertha W. Author, 1890–Unknown.

2 *The Bible.* Proverbs 22:6 (NKJV).

3 Ibid. John 3:16.

4 Ibid. Psalm 78:5–7.

5 Lewis, C.S. *The Chronicles of Narnia.* United Kingdom: HarperCollins Publishers, 1950–56.

6 "Patience." *Music Machine: Fruit of the Spirit.* Sparrow Records, 1977.

7 "Kids under Construction," *Kids under Construction* Audio Cassette Tape. Word Entertainment Music, 1995.

8 Dobson, James. *Bringing up Boys.* Carol Stream, IL: Tyndale House Publishers, 2011.

Chapter 8

1 van der Post, Laurens and Taylor, Jane. Testament to the Bushmen. *Reader's Digest,* November, 1986.

2 *The Bible.* Psalm 18:30.

3 Mead, Margaret. American Anthropologist, 1901–1978.

4 Resnick, Michael D., Bearman, Peter S., Blum, Robert Wm.,

Bauman, Karl E., Harris, Kathleen M., Jones, Jo, Tabor, Joyce, Beuhring, Trish, Sieving, Renee E., Shew, Marcia, Ireland, Marjorie, Bearinger, Linda H. and J. Richard Udry. "Protecting Adolescents from Harm." *Journal of the American Medical Association* 238 (1997): 223–232.

5 *U. S. Bureau of Census, Statistical Abstract of the United States*, 122nd Ed. 2002. Washington, DC: U.S. Government Printing Office.

6 "Turn Around," words and music by Harry Belafonte, Alan Greene and Malvina Reynolds, 1964.

7 *The Bible.* 1 Corinthians 14:40.

8 Neumark-Sztainer, Dianne, Eisenberg, Marla E., Fulkerson, A., Story, Mary, Larson, Nicole. "Family Meals and Disordered Eating in Adolescents." *Archives of Pediatric Adolescent Medicine,* 2008; 162(1):17-22, doi:10.1001/archpediatrics.2007.9.

9 *The Bible.* Proverbs 17:22.

Chapter 9

1 Colton, Charles Caleb. British Sportsman Writer, 1780–1832.

2 Lewin, Tamar. "Screen Time Higher than Ever for Children". http://www.nytimes.com/2011/10/25/us/screen-time-higher-than-ever-for-children-study-finds.html (accessed 7/19/13).

3 Grossman, Dave. *On Killing: The Psychological Cost of Learning to Kill in War and Society.* New York: Littleton Brown & Co., 2010.

4 Grossman, Dave and Gloria DeGaetano. *Stop Teaching Our Kids to Kill: A Call to Action against TV, Movie and Video Game Violence.* New York: The Crown Publishing Group, 1999.

5 *The Bible.* 1 Timothy 6:10.

6 Gelmis, Joseph. "Shoot to Thrill or Shoot to Kill?" *Newsday*, May 11, 1999. Cited in Ruskin, Gary. *Why They Whine: How Corporations Prey on Our Children.* http://www.mothering.com/community/a/why-they-whine (accessed 7/19/13).

7 Henry, Holly K.M. and Dina L. G. Borzekowski. "The Nag Factor:

How Do Children Convince Their Parents to Buy Unhealthy Foods?" http://www.jhsph.edu/news/news-releases/2011/borze-kowski_nag_factor.html (accessed 7/19/13).

[8] Western Initiative Media; Cited in Ruskin, *Why They Whine.* (2nd ref)

[9] McNeal, James U. and C. Yeh. "Born to Shop." *American Demographics* 15: (1993, June): 34–39.

[10] Dobson, James. *The New Dare to Discipline*. Wheaton, IL: Tyndale House Publishers, 1996.

[11] Anderson, Craig A., Carnagey, Nicholas, and Janie. Eubanks. "Exposure to Violent Media: The Effects of Songs with Violent Lyrics on Aggressive Thoughts and Feelings." *Journal of Personality and Social Psychology* 84 (2003): 960–971.

Chapter 10

[1] Herbert, George. British Poet, 1593–1632.

[2] "The Lighthouse," Words and music by Robbie Hinson, 1991.

[3] *The Bible*. Jeremiah 29:11.

[4] Ibid. Hebrews 11:1.

[5] "Jesus, Lover of My Soul," words and music by Paul Oakley. Kingsway's Thankyou Music. 1995.

[6] *The Bible*. Isaiah 40:31.

[7] Ibid. Isaiah 55:8–9.

[8] Ibid. Isaiah 26:3.

[9] Ibid. Philippians 4:6 (MSG).

[10] Ibid. Matthew 6:34 (MSG).

[11] Ibid. Luke 1:37 (MSG).

[12] Ibid. Psalm 16:7–8.

[13] Ibid. Luke 12:6–7.

[14] Ibid. Isaiah 30:15.

[15] Ibid. Romans 12:18.

[16] Ibid. Colossians 3:12 (MSG).

[17] Ibid. Psalm 13:2–3.

[18] Ibid. Psalm 57:1.

[19] Ibid. Psalm 56:3.

[20] Ibid. Psalm 25:4–5.

[21] Ibid. Psalm 94:18–19.

[22] Ibid. Psalm 34:4.

[23] Ibid. Psalm 30:1.

[24] Ibid. Psalm 68:35.

Chapter 11

[1] Cloud and Townsend. *Boundaries with Kids*.

For more resources or to contact Dr. Mumford:
Visit: beyondrubberduckies.com
E-mail: jamumford@beyondrubberduckies.com
Facebook: beyond rubber duckies
Twitter: @beyondduckies